Optimising e-Brand
Profitability

FINANCIAL TIMES

Prentice Hall

In an increasingly competitive world, it is quality
of thinking that gives an edge – an idea that opens new
doors, a technique that solves a problem, or an insight
that simply helps make sense of it all.

We work with leading authors in the fields of
management and finance to bring cutting-edge thinking
and best learning practice to a global market.

Under a range of leading imprints, including
Financial Times Prentice Hall, we create world-class
print publications and electronic products giving readers
knowledge and understanding which can then be
applied, whether studying or at work.

To find out more about our business and professional
products, you can visit us at www.business-minds.com

For other Pearson Education publications, visit
www.pearsoned-ema.com

Pearson
Education

Optimising e-Brand Profitability

Launching, Growing and Protecting Your Brand Online

KRIS WADIA

An imprint of Pearson Education

London ■ New York ■ San Francisco ■ Toronto ■ Sydney ■ Tokyo ■ Singapore
Hong Kong ■ Cape Town ■ Madrid ■ Paris ■ Milan ■ Munich ■ Amsterdam

PEARSON EDUCATION LIMITED

Head Office:
Edinburgh Gate
Harlow CM20 2JE
Tel: +44 (0)1279 623623
Fax: +44 (0)1279 431059

London Office:
128 Long Acre
London WC2E 9AN
Tel: +44 (0)20 7447 2000
Fax: +44 (0)20 7240 5771
Website: www.briefingzone.com

First published in Great Britain in 2001

© Kris Wadia 2001

ISBN 0 273 65333 4

British Library Cataloguing in Publication Data
A CIP catalogue record for this book can be obtained from the British Library.

10 9 8 7 6 5 4 3 2 1

Typeset by Boyd Elliott Typesetting
Printed and bound in Great Britain

The Publishers' policy is to use paper manufactured from sustainable forests.

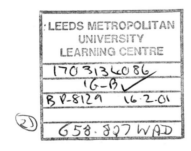

About the author

Kris Wadia is an Associate Partner in the UK Financial Services practice of a global management consultancy firm.

A Chartered Certified Accountant by education, he is also a Member of the Institute of Direct Marketing. His career has included employment with blue-chip multinationals in publishing and financial services in Europe and Asia.

His previous books include the *Asian Direct Marketing Handbook* and *Successful Financial Management*.

Kris has presented insights on the subject of e-Branding and e-Marketing to audiences around the world since 1996.

The author may be contacted at:

www.kriswadia.com

For my family – specially Mom and Dad

Contents

List of tables and figures

Tables

Figures

List of abbreviations

CEO	chief executive officer
CPM	cost per mille (thousand)
CTR	click-through rate
DNS	domain name server
FAQ	frequently asked questions
HTML	hypertext mark-up language
ICANN	Internet Corporation for Assigned Names and Numbers
IP	Internet protocol
ISP	Internet service provider
IT	information technology
PC	personal computer
SSL	secure sockets layer protocol
UDRP	Uniform Domain-Name Dispute-Resolution Policy
URL	uniform resource locator
USP	unique selling proposition
VAD	viewer attention deficit
W3C	World Wide Web Consortium
WAP	wireless application protocol
XML	extensible mark-up language
Y2K	Year 2000

Preface

This Executive Briefing was born from the perceived need for a work that provided knowledge on the subject of e-Branding that could be utilised in a practical manner for increased business profitability.

To do this, knowledge has been drawn from various sources – experience of successful (and failed) strategies, the distilled essence of case studies around the world and leading-edge thinking on the subject. The resulting analyses should be actionable immediately by anyone charged with building and protecting an e-Brand.

In keeping with the generalised nature of the work, not all the insights provided will be applicable to each reader. In fact, some insights might even appear contradictory, yet perfectly logical in the context of businesses with differing needs and circumstances.

Named examples have been intentionally avoided, as fast-changing market conditions could turn today's specialist site into tomorrow's portal.

Persons requiring details of branding theory, the design components of branding or the use of Internet technology for marketing will find other works on these subjects far more enlightening.

This Briefing was always intended for those who asked the questions: how can I use e-Branding to increase revenues, avoid expensive mistakes and optimise the profitability of my business? If the insights – especially those defying conventional wisdom – provide some of the answers, this Executive Briefing will have achieved its objective.

Kris Wadia
www.e-brandoptimisation.com

Acknowledgements

With thanks to the people at the firm who – directly or indirectly – provided the impetus that made this Briefing possible:

- Jon Allaway
- Juan Amador
- Antony M. Badsey-Ellis
- Paul Cantwell
- Simon Daniel
- Keith Haviland
- Antonio Moreira da Silva
- Laurie A. Rasmussen
- Allen Wolpert

and special thanks to Raj Paranandi.

And to those outside the firm – for their time and honest evaluations:

- Anthony Appleby
- Jerome Gudgeon
- Karl Humphreys
- Colette Johndrow
- Chris Jones
- Rob Lugt, Elcel Technology Ltd, roblugt@elcel.com
- Martin McHarg
- Leezily Monastyrski
- M. Raghuram, RAGHU, www.brinjal.com

Prologue

WHAT IS A BRAND?

So what, exactly, is a brand?

Defining a brand is not as easy as it might appear. It depends on whether it is being viewed in a legal, marketing or accounting context. What's more, even within each profession, there is no clear agreement.

Consider the following broad alternatives:

- *Legal* – an identifying mark, symbol, word(s) or combination thereof that identifies one owner's products or services as distinct from another.

- *Marketing* – a personality or image of a product or organisation in the minds of customers based on tangible and intangible attributes derived from promotion or usage.

- *Accounting* – brands are part of the intangible assets and goodwill that can arise from an acquisition and be amortised over their useful economic lives (in the UK).

WHAT IS BRAND EQUITY?

But it is perhaps the concept of brand equity that is of greater interest in a business context. Again, definitions vary, but one could say that brand equity is a term that identifies a brand as a key intangible asset for a business that can now be listed in the balance sheet in countries such as Britain, France and Australia.

The logic that underpins brand equity goes as follows:

- Familiarity with the brand results in ongoing revenue streams, without the requirement for continual advertising support.

- These revenue streams can be obtained at higher profit margins, without having to resort to deep discounting during the course of normal trading activities.

- The combined effect of the above is to monetise the 'equity' which is perhaps the image an established brand has built in users' minds, given their interaction with its promotional activities and repeat usage.

The same principles apply to an e-Brand – the presentation of your brand online – although the execution varies considerably compared with the offline world.

To understand the fiscal significance of brands and e-Brands, consider the league table of brand values in the year 2000 shown in Table 1.1.

Table 1.1	League table of brand valuations	
Rank	*Brand*	*Brand valuation ($bn)*
1	Coca-Cola	72.5
2	Microsoft	70.2
3	IBM	53.2
	Online brands	
38	Yahoo!	6.3
47	AOL	4.5
48	Amazon.com	4.5

Source: Interbrand/Citibank, July 2000.

According to Nick Liddell, a brand valuation consultant at Interbrand, 'at the heart of a brand are trade mark rights'. He continues:

> *Because a brand designates a product or service as being different from competitors' products and services, it establishes an emotional 'pact' between the supplier and consumer and, because of this, brands provide a security of demand that suppliers would not otherwise enjoy if they did not own the brand. This security of demand means a security of future brand earnings, and this is what lies at the heart of brand valuation.*

Launching an e-Brand

Before we go any further let us consider the pervasive nature of brands today.

Originally associated with high society and its expensive accoutrements, brands are no longer the exclusive domain of the wealthy. They form an integral part of the profit-generating arsenal of any form of commercial activity – including illegal ones.

But what if one were to get away from it all – and spend a few days in the brand-free world of Mother Nature. All it would take to shatter this myth would be a backward glance, which would invariably show the brand of the footwear manufacturer clearly stamped on the soil with each and every step taken by the walker.

The focus on brands on the Internet has, similarly, been driven by economic factors. Announcing an Internet brand has been known to add the necessary sparkle to a languishing share price for an existing business – or get a new one off to a flying start.

And with anywhere up to 75 per cent of initial funding being spent on 'building the brand', survival depends on getting the e-Branding strategy and execution absolutely right.

So how does one go about launching, growing and protecting an e-Brand? Is there a 'right' strategy that fits all situations? And to what extent could – or should – an existing brand be leveraged in the virtual world? What name should be used for the online venture? How should the launch marketing be managed?

All these questions – and more – are examined below.

WHY DO BRANDS EXIST?

The answer depends on who you ask!

Brands exist for several reasons – and it is important to understand all of them even before the first strands of an e-Branding strategy are put into place. The answers are also likely to vary depending upon the group being questioned.

The corporate viewpoint

- Brands allow customers to express a preference for a company's products or services at the expense of competitors.
- Revenues are likely to continue even without the ongoing support of advertising or promotional activity.
- A company's branded products or services can retain their higher prices – and profit margins – even in the face of lower priced competitors.

- The brand can be leveraged into new product lines, industries, geographies or market segments without the high level of marketing expenditure that would otherwise be required.

- Employees, trading partners and third-party suppliers are more likely to deal with an established and respected brand.

- Part of the market capitalisation of the business is due to the intangible value attributed to the brand...the greater the perception, the higher the share price.

The customer viewpoint

- Customers are never as familiar with all the products in a single category as the companies that manufacture them. Customers use their preference for a particular brand, therefore, to help guide their purchasing decisions.

- Customers view a product through personalised lenses – i.e. what will this product do for me? This may or may not be consistent with the generic attributes of the product highlighted in advertising and marketing campaigns.

- Customers' perceptions often focus on the intangibles associated with a product and may not always be logical. For example, the packaging of a product may trigger subconscious memories of a favourite birthday gift, resulting in an impulse purchase.

- Customers tend to carry out their own form of segmentation. For example, although a product could be used equally at work and at home, it is never considered for the latter simply because of its overwhelming associations with the person's place of employment.

The brand practitioner viewpoint

- Brands exist solely in the minds of consumers, not in advertising campaigns, on the Web or in retail outlets.

- A greater 'share of mind' is what actually results in an increased 'share of wallet'.

- Brand wars are essentially psychological battles between competitors with the ultimate goal of retaining top-of-mind awareness in customers' minds. This is best achieved through repeated promotion, availability and use of the product or service.

- Famous brands cannot expect to remain at their exalted heights without continual investment or care. Historic triumphs have a habit of being forgotten in the light of current disasters.

■ Recognising changing economic fundamentals is critical. For example, of all the air travel brands that existed before the Second World War, not one survives in its original form today.

UNDERSTANDING THE DIFFERENCES BETWEEN THE REAL AND ONLINE WORLDS

Why the Internet is not a mass market, despite its huge size

There are several reasons, but in decreasing order of practicality, they can be listed as follows:

■ Not everyone is interested in what you have to offer.

■ If they are interested, they may not have access to the online world.

■ If they do, they may still prefer to source your products or services via traditional media, which are easier to use, given their familiarity.

■ If they want to find you on the Internet, they may find it difficult to sift through the sheer volume of information available.

■ Even if they do find you, they may find the Internet culture – especially the absence of helpful humans – unacceptable.

■ The final click needed to place the order may still never happen because they do not know if your ability to deliver their purchases will outlast your ability to remain in business.

It's a new world out there – understand it or fail!

Despite the above, there is a new, profitable online world out there. Failure to understand the differences between the real, tangible world and the online world – and the economic implications of such differences – probably accounts for more business failures than any errors in executing an online strategy.

This extends to the role of the brand online, which is more important than in a physical retail context, as online customers often pay for goods and services up front and have no assurance of delivery – or recourse to live human beings in the event of dissatisfaction.

What's more, brands no longer represent the benefits of a handful of product features, but are complex and intertwined manifestations of product, service and intangibles such as entertainment, or one-upmanship.

Appeal to the new elite

And even the manner of upstaging others has changed. Keeping up with the Joneses – an underlying premise in the early days of branding – is no longer the attraction it once was. In fact, consumers often want to be as different as possible from the Joneses they know. They aim to do this by forming temporary alliances with brands that reflect their 'new' values and self-image. In fact, the typical person dressed for a night out with friends now uses and displays more brands than a street full of advertising billboards.

So, how can an organisation capitalise on these differences to appeal to the online elite? They are an elite of sorts, as they have access to the online world, whereas a substantial portion of the globe still does not.

Some fundamentals haven't changed

Even for the elite, some fundamentals haven't changed. People still want to be richer, happier, healthier, etc., but now they want it at e-Speed! While the technology surrounding them is changing constantly, and new processes add even more communication and service channels, the basic desires of human beings remain constant.

Understanding the differences – and their implications

- Relationships with customers have become one of the key differentiating factors, given that most customers are now faced with a bewildering array of choices in each product category. However, they have a mental limit to the number of choices they can possibly recall. So, it is these relationships that allow the customer to see an offering as a solution, rather than yet another product or service competing for his limited time and attention.

- Another significant difference is that control of the brand relationship has increasingly moved from the supplier to the customer. Multiple touch-points, such as the phone centre and delivery personnel, may no longer be within the direct control of the supplier. When coupled with the availability, low cost and richness of information from external sources, the consumer is no longer reliant on a principal supplier (and a couple of competitors) for input on all purchasing criteria.

- These relationships continue to be threatened, not just by direct and indirect competitors, but also by disintermediation – the act of cutting out middlemen. Of course, a business could always re-intermediate itself, by focusing on personalised, individual customer service and after-sales activities, but these challenges are likely to persist for some time.

- Customers are increasingly sceptical when brands suddenly appear out of nowhere, gain temporary awareness, and disappear just as quickly. This disadvantages e-Brands compared with existing real-world brands, especially if the relationship is expected to endure beyond a one-time purchase – which it must do if the objective is to optimise profitability for the supplier.

- While e-Brands exist, they are expected to grow strong very quickly, and become as relevant as possible to their intended customer base. Yet the measure of success is often not profitability or market share, but market capitalisation, which results in decisions that favour short-term gain over long-term stability.

- Most of the sensory cues related to traditional brand building are not available to online brand marketers, as customers cannot touch, feel or smell the product online – yet! These will increasingly be substituted with multimedia presentations, incorporating video and virtual reality.

- Organisations have to accept the fact that there is nowhere left to hide when things go wrong. Truth will out – often sooner rather than later.

Each of these seismic shifts will be discussed in detail later in this Executive Briefing.

Traditional versus new media – and their marketing implications

Differences between the offline and online worlds are often magnified by the relative strengths and weaknesses of the media used.

Examples of traditional media include press advertising and direct mail, while new media is best represented by the Internet.

This makes it imperative to understand the differences in the media – and the impact they are likely to have on e-Branding campaigns. The mantra – the medium is the message – has long been known, but it has taken the arrival of new media to emphatically demonstrate the significance of that statement.

The marketing message used in traditional media cannot usually be repeated – without adaptation – in the new media, as the channel of communication distorts the message. For example, a picture of a smiling child on a billboard advertising milk powder might be fine – but visitors to the milk powder Internet site are unlikely to be impressed if all they find is the same picture of the child staring back at them. The medium – in this case, the Internet – is expected to offer more, for example contact details of the nearest retail outlet, ingredients, recipes, etc. Because these are missing, the medium has effectively distorted the message.

Used intelligently, however, new media can amplify the features of the product or service being marketed.

Table 2.1 serves as a high-level summary of the key differentiating factors between traditional and new media.

Table 2.1 Key differentiating factors between traditional and new media

Feature	Traditional media	New media
General		
Size advantage	Uneven playing field, exemplified by the differences in the budget available for marketing, which invariably favours larger organisations.	More level playing field, with intelligent use of technology being the main instrument of equalisation. Usually supported by innovative, yet inexpensive, marketing strategies such as broadcast e-mail or viral marketing.
Technical literacy of customers	None assumed or required.	Minimum technical literacy and access to new media required, with the implicit burden of keeping pace with new developments.
Physical attributes	Tangible – allowing promotional material to be stored and responded to at a later date.	Intangible and transient – the site may never be found again if not bookmarked, and even if bookmarked may no longer be available at that location.
Approach	Can be invasive – direct mail arrives at your address uninvited.	Passive until discovered – site is invisible until the visitor arrives.
Frequency	Cyclical/seasonal – lead times involved with print and production usually result in cyclical or seasonal campaigns.	Continuous – the site is live and has to be continually updated and monitored.
Nature of relationship	Broadcast – organisation tells customer what it thinks he or she needs to hear.	Network – customer obtains information from the organisation, its competitors, rating agencies and other purchasers before deciding on action.
Geographic reach	Local or, at most, regional – subject to marketing budget available.	Global – irrespective of whether or not the products and services can be offered on a global basis, the site is accessible from anywhere in the world with a suitable Internet connection (subject to governmental filtering in some countries).
Repetition	Essential – to keep top-of-mind awareness of the key marketing messages.	Offensive – if repeated, e.g. multiple e-mails, or if static, e.g. no new content on the site.
Human involvement	Expected – the norm would be to expect human involvement at all times from the initial sale through to post-sale customer service.	Not expected – except in the event of difficulty with the automated processing of the interaction between the organisation and the customer.

Payment and returns	Expected to pay in advance, with a suitable returns policy should the product/service be unacceptable.	Customer does not expect to pay for anything that can be provided in digital format. Restricted returns policy for non-digital purchases.

Marketing implications

Lead times	Long lead times for creation of marketing material to allow for production, print and mail.	Short lead times as the site is live and often requires existing content to be updated and modified.
Volume of information	Limited by the media used and related production costs.	Virtually unlimited – can be expanded by adding more storage and processing capacity. Important to recognise the perception that volume = comprehensiveness = value worth paying for.
Features	Single, or a few, can be illustrated in a single campaign.	Multiple features can be illustrated within the same campaign.
Involvement devices	Limited to media used, e.g. direct mail can allow for 'pull here', 'scratch this', 'sniff that'.	Limited to technology used – and can include anything from real-time, interactive contests to quizzes, lotteries, etc.
Sensory cues	Touch, taste, smell, e.g. coffee or perfume sample.	Sight and sound – in the form of video and audio, and increasingly virtual reality.
Demonstrations of product features	Simple, usually photographs and illustrations.	Can be as complex and detailed as required with 'cutaways', 3D and virtual reality imagery.
Customers' required actions	One, or a couple at most.	Multiple types of relationships can be established with visitors, e.g. visitor only, registrant for access to greater information, or customer with full trading functionality.
Campaign results	Delayed until responses are received, collated and analysed.	Instantaneous aggregation and analysis of data is possible.

IS THERE A 'RIGHT' STRATEGY?

There is bad news for those looking for a shortcut when building an e-Brand – there is no single 'right' strategy. It is impossible to prescribe a 'one size fits all' solution for all online businesses, as the variables they face – geography, market, industry, infrastructure, customer sophistication, etc. – differ considerably between businesses and countries.

Right strategy or strategy right?

Instead of looking for the 'right' strategy, businesses would be better off getting their strategy right – and the importance of the latter cannot be overstated.

The strategy drives the business model, which determines, among other things, the brand position as expressed through the name and promotional campaigns.

This in turn drives customer expectations, which in the days and weeks immediately after launch, must be managed and satisfied if the brand is to survive beyond the launch phase.

Over time, a clear strategy will manifest itself in the eyes of its target audience as a trustworthy e-Brand, accessible and used by millions around the world.

Start-up or upstart?

Without getting the strategy right, a potentially successful start-up could turn into nothing more than a short-lived upstart.

The sequence of the key start-up criteria influencing e-Brand strategy is often as follows:

- *What is the principal objective?* This could range from obtaining a high market capitalisation to high profitability in a niche sector.
- *What is the starting point?* For an established business, with an existing customer base and strong cash flows, the starting point would be materially different compared with a venture capital funded start-up.
- *What is the 'real' business opportunity?* For example, when a factory owner switches thinking from 'I manufacture safes' to 'I manufacture safety devices, in many shapes and forms, for people to store their valuables', a whole new vista opens up. If the outcome of the thinking requires amendments to an existing real-world model, is the business prepared to change it? Will the existing corporate culture allow such change?
- *Which online business model should be adopted?* Should it be just a new channel or a stand-alone operation? Could it be run as an exchange? Or even an auction model? And what about alliances?
- *What is the time horizon for the strategy?* Often, dot com start-ups find this only extends as far as the next round of funding.
- *How should branding and naming be executed?* Should it be descriptive? Or how about something trendy?
- *Where should the marketing investment be made?* In the real or virtual worlds? Or both? What are the target audiences? Where can they be found?

■ *What form should the 'look and feel' take?* Should it just be a virtual extension of the real-world business? Or should leading-edge audio-visual technology be used?

Which business model?

Entire books have been devoted to the subject of online business models, using terminology that changes every few months.

A 'back to basics' approach would suggest that there are, in the broadest sense, three sets of people who could, individually or jointly, control any business model:

■ buyers

■ sellers

■ interested third parties.

The choice of the base model, or a suitable variant thereof, must be driven by the strategic thinking that preceded it.

But it worked in the US!

Even after the base model has been selected, there remains the issue of whether it should be adopted in its entirety or adapted for the local environment.

The success of a specific business model in the US marketplace should not be taken as the recipe for riches in other parts of the world – as the context is unlikely to be identical.

Broadly speaking, established businesses outside the US should find it easier to catch up with their local dot com competitors, as the latter will be dealing with nascent markets for both venture capital and online customers.

Initial e-Brand parameters

At this stage, it is worth setting out some e-Brand parameters within which to frame the next level of detailed thinking.

■ It is human nature to stick with the familiar, which explains why surveys consistently rate new online-only brands lower than the virtual extensions of established real-world competitors. This offers established firms an opportunity to leverage some of the millions spent on brand recognition efforts – if they can execute the online strategy effectively.

■ The distance between physical retail outlets and the online world may be a lot shorter than it might appear at first glance. Consumers – especially those who are likely to be users of online services – have increasingly been weaned off retail services, as the alternative communication and transactional channels are better, cheaper and easier to use. These include call centres, automatic teller machines, kiosks, interactive voice response services and proprietary (non-Internet-based) online services. Profitable, trust-based e-Brand relationships can, and should, build on this base of partial converts initially.

- Not all brands could justify or benefit exponentially from online exposure. This situation is similar to the real world where certain branded products or services are inappropriate for, say, telemarketing, for reasons ranging from a low sales price per unit to limited geographic availability or regulatory constraints. However, the total absence of an online presence risks being misinterpreted, even by real-world customers, as incompetence and could result in offline sales suffering needlessly.

- Established businesses should consider experimenting with alternatives such as hybrids, which theoretically combine the strengths of an existing offline brand with the freshness and novelty of the online world.

- Radical solutions that challenge conventional thinking – for example, using the Internet to push traffic to retail outlets rather than the other way around – should also be evaluated.

- Entering a totally new arena does hold the attraction of having no competitors – but equally others may have sound reasons for not entering that niche.

- If the commercial objective is to build and sell off a suite of products or a specialist subsidiary, these are better off not being branded with the parent company's name, thereby avoiding confusion and conflict in the future.

- Corporate size is not necessarily a precondition for brand prominence, as the user experience is influenced by several factors – including access, navigation, customer service and community feeling – and not just the sums of money spent on marketing and advertising.

- Cutting corners by simply transferring existing printed marketing collateral to the online presence could be expensive in terms of time, money and brand damage. Print is static, but online media such as the Internet are expected to be interactive. The absence of suitable added value could lead users to feel they are being cheated.

- Wherever possible, the e-Brand should own the customer relationship, irrespective of the medium or partner generating the online visit or the supplier used to service the business. The intrinsic value of the customer relationship is that it can be leveraged into other product, geographic or functional areas, without extensive marketing expenditure.

- In the early days of the Internet, forecasters loudly declared 'content is king'. While they have been less vociferous in recent times, content remains an important component of any e-Brand, and its absence is penalised immediately by users failing to make a repeat visit.

- A strong sense of community within the online presence allows users to feel they are in the company of peers and friends who interact with the same e-Brand. Their recommendations and comments are likely to carry greater credibility than any organisations' promotional messages.

- Future e-Brands are likely to be positioned closer to the corporate or product family level rather than the individual product or service level. This would allow a brand, and its related expenditure, to cover a range of products, especially if they are available on a regional or global basis. A uniform corporate brand reinforcing an extensive product line would imply a stable global entity ready to back its offerings at any time, anywhere in the world.

    Also, fierce competition and the need for rapid market response may force changes to individual product specifications at a fast pace. This may be uncomfortable for existing users who need repeated interactions over an extended period of time to build brand familiarity and loyalty.

Typical corporate first foray

Some key e-Brand parameters were listed earlier. Unfortunately, in the real world, they have to be incorporated into the sequence of events which characterises an established corporation's first foray into the online world.

This sequence is best explained by the typical comments heard around each stage of entry into the online world as listed in Table 2.2.

Table 2.2 The '9As' model

Sequence	Typical corporate comment
Aversion	'We're too big to be affected by this Internet fad and this dot com competitor X.'
Anger	'How dare our customers defect to X, especially after all the service we've given them over the years.'
Acceptance	'We need to launch a website tomorrow. The chairman's son has just told him our competitors have their own website.'
Action	'So, what should we do?'
Atypical behaviour	'No more committees – we need to move at e-Speed – we'll set up a task force instead!'
Attack	'Run some large advertisements reminding our customers we have been in business since 1869 and X may not last beyond next Tuesday.'

Agencies	'Offer everyone we know huge discounts to sell our products, as long as they promise not to stock X's products.'
Alliances	'Let's do deals with everyone we can think of, as long as they promise not to deal with X.'
Acquire or be acquired	'Better get me the telephone number of X's chairman. We need to buy them right now before they can afford to buy us.'

Why a 'vanity site' could cost more than just pride!

A vanity site is an online presence that is set up without a sound underlying commercial strategy and business model. Typical 'justifications' for setting up vanity sites include:

- 'The chairman said so.'

- 'Our major competitor has [or for that matter, has not] got one.'

- 'I read somewhere that if we don't have a site, we can't register our domain name.'

Unfortunately, these sites are likely to cause more harm than good, given their absence of content and functionality.

A discreetly parked domain name (along the lines of 'The future home of …') and some offline contact details would cause less damage than a site littered with amateur graphics, garish colours, mismatched typefaces and typographical errors.

THE IMPORTANCE OF THE RIGHT NAME

An organisation's domain name represents its unique identifier – and it is critical to get it absolutely right at the outset (see Table 2.3).

Table 2.3 Checklist for choosing a memorable domain name

Criteria	Explanation
Unique	Unlikely to be associated with an existing name by conscious association, visual imagery or auditory cues.
Available	This probably creates the greatest hurdle, especially with millions of domain names already having been registered.
Not geography specific	Otherwise, rolling out the brand on a global basis will present difficulties, unless of course the geographic associations are both positive and clearly recognisable as being unique to that region.

Emotionally evocative	Possibly by turning the word(s) into memorable characters based in history or fiction.
Easily pronounceable	Bear in mind that not everyone speaks with the accent of a single country and may read the word with an unintended (and unfortunate) emphasis on the wrong syllables.
Culturally inoffensive	This is one of the most sensitive aspects of domain name selection and will require specialist assistance if viewed on a global basis.
Category descriptor	This is a double-edged sword. While a name with, say, 'cars' in the title will immediately describe the category in which it operates, over time it will be difficult to retain distinction from all the other names with 'cars' in the title as well.
Memorable	The shorter, simpler and clearer the domain name, the greater the chance of it being memorable.
Anagram-safe	The letters of the domain name should not form any unfortunate combination if rearranged.
Not dated	The words should not be selected because they happen to be in fashion at present as this will certainly make the name appear dated within a relatively short period of time.
Avoidance of cliches	Using cliches implies a lack of imagination – or desperation – or both.
Support of strategic vision	The domain name should be representative of the organisation's strategic vision.

Practical precautions

When registering a domain name, obtain all the variants, where relevant and possible. These include the following:

- Top-level domains such as .com. Although .net and .org may be available, these are usually recommended for Internet infrastructure providers and not-for-profit organisations respectively.

- Country- and business-specific domains. In the UK, these would include .co.uk, .ltd.uk, .plc.uk.

- Alternative domains such as .tv and .it if your business operations match these initials, e.g. entertainment or information technology respectively in the above examples.

- Different forms of presenting two or more words, e.g. using hyphenations or abbreviations.

- Possible misspellings of the domain name, e.g. principle and principal.

- Possible alternative spellings of the domain name, e.g. ebrandoptimisation.com and ebrandoptimization.com differ when spelled in the UK or USA.

- Relevant prefixes and suffixes, e.g. 'e-...' or 'buy...'.

- Nicknames and colloquial variations of the name. There is no greater shock than finding an organisation's publicly used nickname being used to drive traffic to an inappropriate site.

- It is now possible to register top-level domain names (currently .com, .net and .org) of up to 67 characters in length, and the full name of the organisation should also be registered. Other domain names cannot exceed 22 characters, excluding the extension.

- The domain name will, by default, be seen globally, so country-specific domains, including those where there are no business operations currently, might still be worth reserving, if only to prevent an entrepreneur cashing in on brand equity created elsewhere.

- There have been discussions related to the implementation of new top-level domains, such as .shop, .firm and .web. Placing advance orders with reputable domain registrars might help an organisation receive its preferred names once these domains are actually implemented, although stricter qualifying criteria are also being discussed to reduce the risk of cybersquatting.

But what if the preferred name has already been taken?

There are a few strategies to adopt, depending on whether or not the business believes it has a strong case for ownership of the name.

- If there is clear evidence of abusive registration of a domain name (e.g. cybersquatting), it may be appropriate to submit a complaint to an approved dispute-resolution service provider. They may be able to conduct expedited administrative proceedings under the Uniform Domain-Name Dispute-Resolution Policy (often referred to as the UDRP) which is followed by all registrars in the .com, .net and .org top-level domains. Details may be obtained from ICANN – Internet Corporation for Assigned Names and Numbers.

- If this is not practical or possible, legal action against the registered owner of the site, and their Internet service provider acting as the publisher, might achieve the desired results.

- The situation is more difficult when two similarly named individuals or businesses both want the same domain name. Generally, the principle of 'first come, first served' will apply.

- The next step would be to consider trying some of the variations on the name as explained earlier.

- An offer could be made to purchase the domain name from its current, legal, registered owner.
- A joint venture could be considered, whereby the owner shares the domain name with the organisation requiring it, and obtains a return on the investment through a share of the joint venture's profits.

Timing issues

- If proof of urgency in registering domain names was ever needed, it can be found in the fact that business rumours of impending mergers, acquisitions or divestitures result in an instant rash of domain name registrations by cybersquatters around the world. The reverse also applies, with some business intelligence agencies existing solely to monitor domain name registrations and infer potential market-moving developments.
- Branding and naming consultancies have reconfigured their processes to work at the same speed as clients requiring brand creation, validation and registration services. They should be brought into the strategic thinking process as soon as possible, as their input will influence the market-facing component of any strategic thinking.
- Some timing issues have to be taken in context. Artificially engineered domain names, which do not exist in the language today, will take some time to acquire meaning. Their success or failure can only realistically be measured several months or years after their creation.

Which is best – an existing or a new name?

There is no prescriptive answer to this question, although it is possible to calibrate the response as follows – the greater the similarity between a new online operation and its existing real-world counterpart, the greater the value and possibility of leveraging the existing brand.

Three categories of models emerge from this thinking:

- *New channel* – positions the online presence as just another communication and transaction channel. It implies that the customer enjoys the same level of functionality and service in both the online and offline worlds. e-Branding usually takes the form of 'ExistingBusiness.com'.
- *Separate operation* – positions the online presence as a separate operation, but is clearly sub-branded to show it as part of a group with roots in the real world, i.e. the 'trust' is borrowed from an existing operation. e-Branding often takes the form of 'NewBusiness.com, a subsidiary of ExistingBusiness'.

- *Internet-only operation* – positions the entity as having only an Internet presence, implying that it is expected to succeed or fail on its own merits, as its real-world parent may not operate in the same market space, or may be using an entirely different revenue model. This type of operation will have to build trust by repeated usage of the service, and should bring to bear all the advantages of the online world – which include low cost and global access, among others. e-Branding usually takes the form of 'NewBusiness.com' with little or no mention of 'ExistingBusiness'.

Names based on market positioning

Sometimes a predetermined market positioning will drive the strategic thinking and influence the choice of name. For example:

- *Lifestyle brand* – this usually represents an aspirational style of living rather than a specific product.
- *Challenger brand* – a position taken by a brand and its owner as aiming to offer better value than the established leader in a given market space. This may either manifest itself as a serious contender for the top spot or proffer opportunistic jibes at the slower reaction times of the larger, more cumbersome, leader.
- *Customised solution* – this positioning helps customers to cut through the product choice clutter of several million alternatives currently available on the Internet. It positions the brand as being the customers' friend, helping them make an independent choice from a mind-boggling selection. It is particularly useful in categories that are swamped by similar sounding descriptive names.

Adopt an orphan

One rarely considered, yet potentially lucrative, alternative is to consider adopting an orphan brand.

Loosely defined as a brand that has fallen from greatness due to lack of investment, changing customer preferences, etc., an orphan brand should still resonate with consumers who have used it in the past, or those who hanker after a return to the 'good old days'. It goes without saying that research should confirm that the 'good old days' do not include behaviours that would be considered inappropriate in today's world.

Although this may offer a head start in the form of rose tinted memories, it rarely offers any guarantees of ongoing success, unless new customers also buy into the nostalgia.

Orphans may have lost their trade mark protection given the passage of time, or may have to be purchased from their former owners. Increasingly, as large corporations streamline their brand portfolios, focusing only on their strongest brands, they create new orphans, which may have greater value to a third-party entrepreneur than to their current owner.

That looks pretty – what is it?

A logo is a visual representation of a brand name and is just as important as the online world increasingly offers opportunities for visually led campaigns.

Common logo design faults mirror those made when selecting a name – using visuals that are likely to be dated, geography-specific associations, unreadable typefaces and culturally inappropriate symbols.

An intelligently designed logo can be invaluable – especially when customers need help with purchasing decisions and are looking either for a known, trusted friend or a new guide that inspires trust and respect.

A rose by any other name would not smell as sweet

So, how can the choice of name be validated to ensure it is the right one to meet predefined strategic objectives?

Take the 10-second test. Stop people in the street at random, and give them a card with the name and logo of the proposed online operation. Allow them to stare at it for a full 10 seconds – which is roughly the amount of time a casual visitor is likely to stop at an Internet site before deciding whether or not to leave. Then flip the card over and ask three searching questions:

- Can they guess the nature of business of the online operation?
- Can they remember the name?
- Can they describe the logo?

The greater the number of blank responses, the harder it will be to build an e-Brand using that name and logo combination.

DESIGN AND NAVIGATION OF YOUR ONLINE PRESENCE

VAD is bad

VAD or viewer attention deficit is the single largest enemy of an e-Brand once the visitor has actually arrived at the site. Combating this requires an understanding of its causes – and potential remedies.

■ *Focusing on external rather than internal processes* – online presences often reflect internal departmental requirements rather than visitors' needs. So it is hardly surprising that millions of visitors leave behind abandoned online shopping carts, incomplete application forms and, worst of all, a bad impression of the organisation. Thinking about the online presence through the mind – and likely behaviour patterns – of a visitor will go some way towards reducing this problem.

■ *Delivering the promise, not just the product or service* – an e-Brand is more than just an attractive-looking visual entity. It is the full set of customer interactions and emotional reactions to all touch-points, from the initial order on the Internet to physical delivery.

■ *First-time visitor fears* – understanding the sequence of real or imagined hurdles a first-time site visitor has to clear before they feel comfortable with the e-Brand is invaluable (see Table 2.4). Generally speaking, the quicker and clearer they can see the responses to their questions, the more likely they are to become customers.

Table 2.4 First-time visitor fears and recommended response

First-time visitor question	Recommended response
'What's in it for me?'	Summary listing of all benefits of the site with ability to drill down to details if preferred; special offers for a limited time or select group of visitors; guided tour demonstrating highlights of the site.
'What is my personal risk in obtaining the proposed reward?'	Limited requirement to divulge personal information until a sample has been tried successfully – unless required by regulatory or security concerns, which should be explained clearly.
'Can I trust the organisation behind the online presence?'	Easy to find and clearly understandable security, privacy and trading policies; emphasis on relationships with real-world parent companies and key trading partners; registration with key government agencies.
'How successful is the organisation likely to be in the long term?'	Evidence of growth; press clippings; stock quote; favourable analysts' reports.
'If I returned, would I find anything new or different?'	Clearly defined 'What's New' section; hints of impending new releases or developments; offering a 'keep me posted' facility via a permission-based, opt-in e-mail list.
'Should I recommend them to anyone else?'	Ability to forward proprietary site content by e-mail to a friend; recommend site to others; rate the site; complete online questionnaire.

Successful design principles

The checklist below should cover the key design principles to be followed when creating a successful online presence and a powerful e-Brand.

- *Interview founders and key personnel* who were responsible for the genesis of the business proposition to understand – in their own words – what they expect the brand to accomplish.

- *Study all the documentation available*, from the business plan to the marketing strategy, to ensure the proposed site will be consistent with these objectives.

- *Start with the end in mind* – bear in mind the online presence is a living, growing entity that will need to be constantly updated. By visualising what the site will look like two years later, potential design constraints can be avoided.

- *Emphasise the unique selling proposition* – what is it that makes this e-Brand different from all others? Also, be careful to distinguish between elements that are taken for granted – such as ease of navigation – and those that are unique to the e-Brand. Creating an online presence to minimum design standards is no longer enough.

- *Consistency is king* – keeping the offline and online messages consistent will allow visitors and customers to form a cohesive picture of the brand proposition in their minds and act upon it with their wallets.

- *Elegant simplicity* – restrict text to just two families of typefaces and use other subtle devices such as size, shading, italicisation and colour to indicate emphasis, where necessary. Mixing multiple typefaces makes the online presence appear amateurish and, worse, illegible.

- *Clash of colours* – sometimes existing corporate colours may not translate effectively to the Internet. In that case, a strategic decision has to be made – is it acceptable to have two similar looking presences, or should the real-world presence be changed to fit its new online equivalent? Also, by using only 'Web-Safe' colours, users should see the site in broadly the same colour scheme as that intended by the designer.

- *Allow for missing pictures* – some users prefer to switch off graphics as it allows for reduced downloading times and faster movement across the Internet. Using 'Alt Tags' effectively will allow them to see the text equivalent of the graphic, and can also help increase the ranking of the site with most search engines (a subject covered later in this Briefing).

- *Stripped down senses* – in the real world, designers can make use of all five human senses: sight, sound, touch, taste, smell. Online, the predominant sense employed is sight – requiring a whole new understanding of design principles.

- *The sound of silence* – this is best replaced with the jingle of the cash register, preferably when Internet technology allows the implanting of memorable audio cues, such as jingles, in perfect harmony with their visual counterparts. Currently, on older computers, or those using slower modems, the result could appear similar to a badly dubbed foreign movie. Also, bear in mind that visitors may not necessarily be familiar with the language chosen, and that universally understood musical cues might be more effective with global audiences.

- *What does the future hold?* While this is a near impossible question to answer, certain technologies have entered the mainstream. These include WAP and XML – and technology also exists to allow the online presence to be accessed anywhere from a mobile phone to a dishwasher. Although it is unlikely that consumers will use their dishwasher for serious online banking in the near future, the possibility has design implications. Some corporations have adopted a trend of using only a visual logo, without any text, as their brand name, which may present difficulties in the future.

- *Designing for awards or rewards?* This has been the perennial conflict between external design houses, whose creative geniuses are driven by industry awards, and hard-nosed marketers, who demand measurable results that drive corporate rewards. Often the two are inconsistent, with designers preferring wide open spaces which make the site look 'elegant' and marketers furious with the under-utilisation of prime real estate and failure to convey their key marketing messages in a forceful manner. The solution – make the requirements crystal clear to any designers, and only hire those whose previous work suggests an understanding of the importance of generating responses, conversion to customers and sales.

The smartest designers create online presences for their dumbest users!

That's because these designers make no assumptions about the technical competence of online users and keep the technology behind their presence well within the reach of their target audience.

They also don't make assumptions about user navigation, e.g. that users will automatically know what they are supposed to do, when and where. They recognise the navigation system as being one of the key variables that determines the success or failure of an online presence.

That's because users constantly have to interact with the navigation system in order to achieve their objectives within a given site. If effective, it will be virtually invisible to the end user, but will leave an impression of a friendly, well-managed organisation (see Table 2.5).

And if they feel tempted to try something radical which may turn the online presence into a navigation nightmare, they can conduct a simple search to see if it has been tried before. Entire websites are dedicated to the subject of offensive and annoying web pages, often with convenient hyperlinks to real-life examples.

Table 2.5 Key components of an effective navigation system

Component	Intended result
Usability	Ability to distinguish links from other non-hyperlinked graphics; all elements operational and reacting exactly as expected; ability to use text-based instructions if graphics switched off.
Consistency	The cornerstone of good navigation, wherein the same elements appear in the same place on each page, and in each section. Consider the following anchor locations which have become the 'de facto' norm for the Web: ■ navigation on the top left; ■ globals (which appear on each page) on the top and bottom of each page; ■ banner advertising at the very top of the page; ■ disclaimers and risk warnings in fine print at the bottom of the page. When users find these elements in these places, they relax and focus on the content of the site instead.
What's next	Never leave users to guess what's going to happen next or how long the process is likely to take. Tell them – up front – with progress updates as they go along.
1, 2, 3	Break down larger processes into simpler steps. Keeping it as simple as 1, 2, 3 has its benefits in that users are more likely to start – and complete – a process if it has been broken into smaller, more digestible chunks.
Intentional redundancy	Allow more than one way for a user to achieve a particular objective. This redundant navigation has its uses – it highlights the versatility of the site and draws attention to the key features that get visitors to return again and again.
Location	Demonstrate location within the site always, allowing the user to see, at a glance, how they can move up the hierarchy to the home page if required.
Access	Use the five ways of managing information – location, alphabetical, time, category, hierarchy – to ensure that access is easily obtainable from any page on the site to any other page within three clicks or less.

Interaction	Use mouse-overs or roll-overs to ensure a suitable text explanation appears when the cursor is held over selected graphical elements. These can be supplemented by audio-visual cues, where appropriate.
Call to action	If there is a specific action the user needs to take, make this obvious. Explain the benefits of taking the step or outline the loss if the action is not taken.
Contact information	This should be available from every single page on the site and could form part of the global elements that appear either at the top or bottom of each page, or in the same place in every left-hand side navigation menu.
Up and down	Allow for easy return to the top of each page where the major navigation icons reside. When important information is contained 'below the fold' (i.e. below the visible portion of the screen) which really should be seen, guide the user through a text or visual explanation, even though a vertical scroll bar may already be in place.
Home page	Access to the home page could form part of the global elements that appear either at the top or bottom of each page.
Growth	Changes and updates will be necessary over time. If well structured, a site could accommodate an increase in the number of pages without affecting the core navigation elements, or requiring a complete redesign every few weeks.

Creativity is great – within limits

Creativity is great – unless it results in the creation of an unusable, e-Brand-damaging online presence, designed to appeal only to its creators. A rainbow's worth of colours, vast open tracts of white space, and download times reaching eternity are just some of the consequences of unbridled creativity.

Instilling a little discipline into the process will add an element of sanity. The discipline can take the following forms:

- *Always use a grid* – these non-existent vertical and horizontal lines simply exist to ensure that everything from the home page onwards appears organised and that visitors and users are effectively trained to look for certain items in the same location every time.

- *Insist on unity* – this has been achieved if all the elements on a page look like they belong together.

- *Keep a sense of balance* – this allows all elements on a page to look as if they are in equilibrium. This does not mean equal – equilibrium can just as easily be demonstrated by, say, concentric circles of varying depths of colours from the inside outwards.

- *Don't blow it out of proportion* – unless there is a deliberate attempt at humour, sticking a large nose on the photograph of your CEO alongside a welcome message is unlikely to inspire confidence among first-time visitors.
- *Play it safe* – well, at least stick to 'Web-Safe' colours. These are the 216 (of the 256) colours that can be handled by most display systems currently in use, and are formed from certain combinations of the three primary additive colours – red, green and blue.

And what if your designer refuses to accept these minimum disciplines, citing artistic differences? Simple – get another designer!

Great team – but who is supposed to do what?

Someone is going to have to do the work to get the online presence built. Who will be in the build team? Who owns the project? Who has the right to contribute to the project? Who can insist upon changes?

All these questions – and more – are answered below, but first it is useful to note that there are three groups of people who should never be allowed to have exclusive control of the online presence. Here's how each group perceives the other two:

- *IT* – this group is keen to test out the latest technology, irrespective of whether or not it is available to users of the online system, and often has scant regard for business results.
- *Marketing and design* – this group has constantly changing requirements, none of which is clearly defined, and is constantly disappointed at IT's ability to deliver.
- *Board of directors* – this group would like the site to have a corporate focus, with sections for investors and the media, and is often remote from the intricacies and day-to-day realities which afflict its staff.

What's needed is a team of specialists, which should include, among others:

- *Online champion* – this role owns the online presence and has ultimate authority over what can, and cannot, appear on the site.
- *Site coordinator* – this role liaises across all departments of the organisation to ensure that changes in one portion of the site are notified to all relevant departments likely to be affected, and that the downstream impact of the changes is minimised.
- *Content authoriser* – this role controls all the content on the site, ensuring it is accurate and free of typographical errors and is constantly updated to keep the site appearing fresh.

- *Technology development specialist* – this role is responsible for selecting the initial and ongoing technical architecture and development tools and setting quality thresholds for speed of development, reliability and maintenance.

- *Technology maintenance specialist* – this role is responsible for ensuring the site is functional 24 hours a day, 365 days a year, that all links are fully operational, and that data on visitor activity is collated, analysed and made available to all relevant personnel.

- *Visual and navigation designer* – this role ensures a site is aesthetically pleasing in addition to being functional, and that it can be effectively navigated.

- *User experience tester* – this role looks for constant improvements to the user experience, using comments from visitors, along with site statistics, to identify and eliminate blockages and dead-ends.

Smaller businesses may need personnel to assume more than one role until growth justifies splitting up the work among newly hired hands.

Brand ownership – top down or bottom up?

The top-down approach to brand ownership requires the specialist site building and maintenance team to report to the brand champion – who could be the CEO of the organisation or a specialist brand manager.

The brand champion would lay out clear guidelines for the use of the brand – to be followed by all employees – but only if the brand champion leads by example. However, there should be a clear path for rapidly evaluating exceptions, especially if there was some tactical advantage to be gained.

In large organisations with multiple brands owned by different brand managers, competition could result in one brand winning in the market, even at the expense of other brands owned by the organisation. While this may be acceptable, it could also result in conflicting messages and change requests to the online champion – and conflict resolution rules must be in place from the outset.

Bottom-up ownership of the brand could provide the impetus for the creation of 'intrapreneurs' – entrepreneurs within an established company. Giving them a base support structure and letting them try out a pilot programme could be a low-cost and low-risk alternative to generating new e-Brands. Once the trial has proved to be successful, it could be set up as a separate online operation in its own right.

Talk is cheap

The bottom-up approach has a significant drawback – a multiplicity of ideas from eager employees, most of which are actually unworkable.

A possible solution that allows sound ideas to rise to the surface could be to insist on written suggestions using a standard template. The template would ask the employee to:

- specify how the suggestion would help improve the e-Brand;
- prove the feasibility and practicality of the suggestion;
- assess the impact on other departments;
- specify the replacement text that would accompany changes on the site;
- indicate who would maintain the changed version of the site.

The roots of this approach lie in the lessons learned from establishing company-wide databases. If employees were asked an open-ended question about the data elements they wished to collect in a database, the list would be virtually endless.

However, when required to calculate the cost/benefit ratio of collecting each data element compared to its use, and including the cost and timeliness of updates and maintenance, the number of requirements correctly falls to the bare essentials.

Understand the effort involved

All persons who come into contact with the specialist site building team should understand the concerted – and coordinated – effort that goes into building and maintaining an online presence.

This is particularly true of the brand champion who should obtain an education, in some depth, of the advantages and limitations inherent in each of the technologies and processes involved. For example:

Multimedia components:

- typography
- visuals
- animation
- audio
- video.

Programming components:

- forms and questionnaires
- search engines
- hyperlinks
- online ordering

- payment
- inventory
- accounting
- security
- integration with customer service call centre.

Invisibility equals success

A site visit can be considered successful when the visitor has not been forced to understand the underlying dynamics such as technology and navigation but has focused exclusively on the content and services available.

If visitors intuitively know where they are on the site, what they are supposed to do next and where to find relevant information, they end up with a favourable impression of the e-Brand and will pay the ultimate compliment – returning to the site!

LAUNCH MARKETING YOUR ONLINE PRESENCE

Before spending anywhere up to 75 per cent of all initial funding on a 'do or die' launch marketing blitz, it is worth recognising a few launch marketing-related truisms.

Brand awareness does not equal brand strength

If the ultimate goal is to build a brand that will last beyond next Tuesday, then an all-out marketing assault is unlikely to be the solution. All that does is buy temporary brand awareness – not brand loyalty or strength, which only arises through continued use of the product or service over time, and having a pleasant customer experience on each occasion.

Limit the wish list

Every organisation dreams of having the perfect site at launch – supported by a memorable marketing campaign that integrates both offline and online media. The reality is that cost and time pressures will force choices to be made – often boiling down to those capable of implementation before a predetermined launch date.

It is essential to identify the critical factors that can kill an online presence even before it is born – problems with bandwidth, domain name registration or operating environments being just a few. Focusing on these, without being distracted by the wish list, usually proves to be very difficult, but the launch stage demands a cool head rather than a warm heart.

Focus your reputation on predetermined targets

Despite the Internet being a global medium, it is neither wise nor practical to assume an e-Brand can only be successful if it is used by every person with an Internet connection.

The key to launch success is to identify and target a limited number of niche categories, and focus time, energy and money exclusively in their direction. If conducted successfully, this base will help extend the reputation with wider target audiences while providing an ongoing revenue stream.

You never get a second chance to make a good first impression

This is particularly true of the Internet, where every technological or process hiccup, especially at the launch stage, invites the derision of the national press.

In the headlong rush to be 'first to market', websites are often made inaccessible by blockages caused by poorly estimated demand. Processing delays often take the gloss off attractive (and expensive) introductory offers. Such self-inflicted injuries serve only to delay the building of the e-Brand.

The problem arises because estimating demand at launch remains a difficult mix of art and science. If estimated at a point greater than reality, expensive computer power remains under-utilised. If estimated lower than the actual demand, bottlenecks prevent access to interested parties and customers face frustrating delays. Subject to the available budget, err on the side of caution.

A single sale might need double the marketing expenditure

Some product categories or underdeveloped online markets are likely to require double the amount of marketing expenditure to acquire a single sale. That's because they have to make two sales – first, educating people in the concept of purchasing that product category online, and second, making the purchase at their site.

Use a combination of online and offline media

Using both offline and online media for launch marketing, with an integrated campaign, creates a virtuous circle, with awareness in the offline world being supplemented by a call to action from campaigns using online media.

The resulting synergistic uplift in response rates would not have been possible from separate campaigns in separate media at separate times.

The penalty for e-Speed might be death!

It is unlikely that an organisation would mail an incomplete direct mail brochure or supply a half-finished product. Yet, day after day, millions of real-world customers are being migrated to e-Channels before they are ready – all in the name of e-Speed.

Damage to the organisation's reputation and e-Brand will invariably outstrip any competitive or financial advantage a premature launch could have generated.

Cooperative teaming, but individual decision making

Rapidly changing business landscapes create a pressure cooker type environment, especially around the launch stage of an e-Brand. These compressed timelines mean that all relevant internal departments and external marketing agencies must cooperate and coordinate to reduce the possibility of a disaster. Yet, when it is time to make a decision, it has to be the responsibility of a single individual, or deadlines will invariably be compromised.

This style of working will also reveal which employees (or support service providers) have not made the mental switch from the real world to the online world. This is most commonly illustrated in the 'can't do' attitude of the former and the 'it's done' attitude of the latter.

Don't mistake apathy for loyalty

Any assumptions that a given percentage of the existing bricks and mortar customers will migrate to the new Internet presence – because 'they have been with us for the last 20 years' – are likely to be flawed.

Customers have been known to remain with their existing supplier, not because they are pleased with the service or the offerings, but because they perceive the effort needed to transfer as being more painful than their current irritations.

Cost of online entry

When an offline business enters the online world for the first time, it faces material issues, some of which could be negative. Understanding these in advance will help extract greater value from launch marketing activities.

- *Channel conflict* – will business currently done through another channel, especially third-party intermediaries, fall off at a rate faster than new online acquisitions?

- *Cannibalisation* – will the migration of existing real-world customers to the online presence jeopardise overall profit margins and even the continued existence of the offline operation?

- *Commoditisation* – as consumers increasingly get access to better and more timely information, will they see this organisation as just another product choice rather than their default supplier?

- *Shortsightedness of Web 'pure plays'* – who misprice products and services in search of a share of eyeballs (not share of wallet) to justify their market capitalisations. They will eventually discover that, when it comes to renewals, customers expect to be bribed all over again. Will their savage discounting only serve to wound the entire marketplace? Can the organisation's online presence position itself above the fray – for example, as a premium service?

- *Spectacular Web failures* – which taint all e-Brands in that market sector, at least for a while. Will the beneficiaries be the quality brands in the real world, retaining their existing customers for longer?

Where's the marketing plan?

At the date of launch, the marketing plan, created alongside the business plan that generated the funding, often bears no relationship to reality.

At a minimum, though, it would still be useful to put the following in writing, if only to measure the gap between stated intentions and commercial reality.

- What are the strategies and business models being used?

- What is the unique selling proposition (USP) of the business, and how soon is it likely to be replicated or bettered by a competitor?

- Which corporate, product or service weaknesses are known, or are likely to become known, to customers and competitors? These could include, for example, the absence of a customer service team.

- What are the organisation's 'hidden' strengths – and could these be made more widely known in the marketplace?

- Is it possible to launch with the product or service that is likely to generate the greatest return? Or do market conditions require a loss leader?

- Who are the intended customers and where, precisely, can they be found? What is the cost per acquisition likely to be? How long will it take to acquire the initial targets?

- What resources will be called upon, both internally and externally, to make the launch a success?

- How will success be measured? Where and how is the raw data for measurement likely to be captured?

- Who has the authority to change the marketing direction and what criteria would trigger such a change?

Avoid advertising assumptions

- The presence of experienced advertising professionals as senior members of the team responsible for launch marketing often leads to a substantial portion of the budget being spent on advertising-related activities by default, even though this may not be ideal in some cases.

- Few online entrepreneurs are marketing experts, and it is reasonable for them to turn to advertising agencies for advice. Often, the only solution offered is a 'cool' advertising campaign, backed by a massive media spend. Again, this may not be the appropriate solution for the client.

- Some advertising campaigns appear to be aimed at venture capitalists rather than potential customers. This invariably affects the style, content and physical location of the campaigns, and leaves potential customers with conflicting messages when the next wave, directed at them, eventually arrives.

- The continued use of the '.com' suffix in advertising campaigns runs the risk that the suffix is the last thing to be mentioned and remembered, and not the actual site address. This has been borne out in surveys which show very low unaided recall for any dot com-related advertising, despite huge media spends on creative campaigns.

Sanity checks can prevent insane spending

Immediately before launch, it would be useful to run a series of sanity checks. These are aimed at ensuring the marketing budget is spent in an optimum manner.

- Take the tone test – select a random number of text messages from personal websites and from corporate websites. Mix these and then reread them. Text from the personal websites should be easily identifiable by its human tone, signifying friendliness, warmth, fun and other positive associations. Compare this with corporate websites, some of which appear to have been written by a committee of robots. Rework the tone of the organisation's online presence, if necessary.

- During the launch stage, an e-Brand will be pulled in several, often conflicting, directions. These include corporate funding requirements, response to competitors, geographic limitations, regulatory constraints and others. The purpose of the sanity check is to keep any knee-jerk reactions to a minimum, as the underlying circumstances are likely to exist only in the short term, but a disproportionate response could damage an e-Brand over the long term.

Bookmark the brain, not just the browser

Given that customers can withdraw from an Internet site at a moment's notice, it is better to bookmark their brain in addition to their browser.

As always, this is achieved through bringing them into contact with the e-Brand in a manner that provides solutions for their needs, and offers an above-average experience at each touch-point in the offline and online worlds.

The results can be amazing. For example, retail sales often rise because customers can look up information, directions, bargains and operating hours on the retail store's Internet site before making their purchases in person.

And how can this success be measured?

It could be assumed that if the corporate name enters the language and represents its product category – for example, Xerox has come to mean photocopying – then it has achieved its objective of bookmarking the brain. However, once a trade mark becomes the generic term for its product category, it could become unprotectable by law, and require a considerable spend in corrective advertising.

Growing an e-Brand

FUEL AND STEERING FOR THE GROWTH ENGINE

Growing an e-Brand is possibly the most difficult of the three stages in the e-Brand life cycle – offering neither the excitement of the launch nor the stability of the protection phase.

Yet, the execution of the growth strategy will determine whether the e-Brand is to join the list of one-hit wonders or go on to become a sustainable success.

The principles that should provide the fuel and steering during the growth phase are covered in greater detail below.

PRINCIPLES AND PRACTICE OF GROWTH

Acquiring the customer is just the start

Organisations forget, all too often, that acquiring the customer is only the first step in a long relationship building process. Initial interactions between the customer and the new online presence will, by and large, determine the duration and the tone of the relationship.

Despite this, organisations often engage in complex and expensive customer acquisition programmes, only to ignore these same customers immediately upon enrolment. Communications designed to smooth the 'settling in' process are likely to repay their modest investment several times over.

Dialogue, not monologue

Organisations will have to learn to engage in regular, two-way, non-sales communication with customers – and not just offer a one-way diet of sales offers. This means learning to listen – and act upon the findings. Employees will have to walk, talk and live the brand values their product or service espouses, as customers now have the facility to broadcast news of empty or broken promises.

What's in it for me?

Once online, customers and visitors are keen to find an answer to this burning question, which is implicit in every site visit. It is a safe assumption that business resulting from the online presence will be in inverse proportion to the amount of space devoted to messages from the chairman, especially on the home page. The closer the answer is aligned with the visitors' key motivators, the greater the likelihood of the initial visit turning into a long-term relationship.

Maybe next time?

Lack of immediate sales should not be viewed as a total write-off. If the visitor had a pleasant experience with the brand, it may have added value that is either being monetised in a retail environment or being stored for use in the future. For example, a visit that resulted in the user obtaining helpful guidance for cleaning carpets could result in a retail sale. Alternatively, the visitor could return for further guidance at a later date and make an online purchase at that time.

Earning your share of the customer's wallet

Most customers select from a repertoire of brands in any given category. Of course, the greater the purchases of your brand, the greater your share of their wallet. Wherever possible, attempts should be made to cross-sell some other product, service or information from the organisation to build an increased share of mind at a corporate or product family level. This reduces, but does not eliminate, the possibility of a brand being replaced by another in the repertoire.

The two stages of online grief

In the real world, the grief felt by an individual on being informed of a terminal illness usually follows five stages – denial, anger, bargaining, depression and acceptance. For visitors to an online presence, there are only two stages or fewer.

- *Denial* – inability to access a site or extended download times often means that the visitor will not return to the site for a long time – if ever.
- *Anger* – at not finding any valuable content or being trapped by poor navigation also means that online shopping carts are likely to be abandoned, along with the site.

There are no further stages, given the sheer volume of online competition and the ability to switch suppliers with the click of a mouse.

Time is money – and the supply is limited

The amount of time an individual spends online is limited by factors ranging from wanting to spend time with the family through to the cost of remaining online. In practical terms, this means that five minutes spent at site X has effectively deprived all other sites from being visited by the same individual for those five minutes.

Success in growing an e-Brand derives from respecting those five minutes and ensuring visitors spend them as productively as possible – resulting in mutual benefit. One major time waster – and to be avoided at all costs – is taking up valuable space on the home page with navel-gazing mission and vision statements from the founder. Frankly, few people care whether 'this organisation believes in the honesty of purpose that results in the creation of value-added services, intent on relieving humanity from its great burdens'.

Another aspect of the importance of time can be expressed in terms of urgency. In the online world, a requirement for newsworthy information results in a flood of visitors, all of whom expect answers right now – not even a few minutes later. While this is unlikely to be the case on non-time-sensitive sites, this pattern of behaviour has reduced the tolerance levels of information seekers to an absolute minimum. They may be prepared to wait for the printed version in their search for analysis, but insist on having rapidly changing data available online when they arrive.

Think global, act local

An online presence, adapted to local language and customs, is likely to attract more visitors and revenue than a 'global' site.

This does not simply mean translating a site from one language to another – other areas requiring consideration include local management plans, technology constraints, language nuances, and regulatory requirements, among others.

All of these have to be offset against the cost of 'localising' the online presence, which might also require the brand to be adapted, preferably without compromising its size, shape or colours.

The localisation will have passed the litmus test if users feel it represents the best efforts of a locally based organisation rather than a downgraded version of a global site – a perception that cannot be determined from a distant head office.

There is also a balance to be struck between the content that appears on the global and local sites. Placing global content on the local site might be seen as pretentious, while placing local content on the global site would be irrelevant to a large number of visitors and users.

Employees are the new brand champions, but are they qualified?

If the employees of an organisation cannot articulate the values of the brand they work for, is it reasonable to expect customers to be able to do so, given their greater distance from the day-to-day operation of the brand?

As a first step, employees should be educated about brand values, and asked whether they genuinely believe them to be true or just a series of fine sounding words strung together. If employees buy into the proposition, they are more likely to be advocates for the brand in their dealings with customers.

The brand message can be reinforced by applying the same standards used for Internet site development and maintenance to the corporate intranet. Employees should also be able to easily locate e-Brand-related messages from the corporate intranet and comment on areas where they feel it is being damaged. Where possible, even temporary staff should be given a quick briefing on the e-Brand values before they commence work.

Don't turn your customer into a prospect

Not communicating with the bricks and mortar customer base for fear of cannibalising existing profitable business does, however, leave them open to capture by other online competitors.

If the first time a customer hears about an organisation's new online service is through a press advertisement, they will choose to view it through the eyes of a prospect – not a loyal customer. In effect, they would see the organisation's online service as one of many choices available to them, rather than the default option, and trust would have to be built all over again.

When migrating real-world customers to an organisation's e-Channel, it is important not to sell to them. Instead, make them feel special by giving them advance notice of the availability of the channel and the efforts planned by the organisation to make their transition a smooth one.

Invite some of them to offer their insights on the new service and, where data protection regulations allow, pre-fill their online application forms with data already available in the offline world, so as to save them the task.

If the migration is to be incentivised, avoid price discounting if possible as this can be matched, or bettered, by competitors. Focus on things customers could obtain only from their current supplier – such as information or service.

Tame the volatility of demand

Even during the growth phase of an e-Brand, demand for the service is likely to remain highly volatile. Yet this same volatility, at peak times, results in restricted or delayed access to the site, which puts off visitors and customers.

Internally generated volatility can, and should, be controlled. If a particular campaign is proving more successful than expected, future media runs should be reduced until the volatility subsides. While this runs counter to most real-world thinking on the subject, it is preferable not to have someone visit the site (with a neutral impression) than a visitor who cannot access it (creating a negative impression).

Keeping technical and bandwidth capacity one step ahead of current requirements, either internally or through a bureau service, might be expensive, but is the only realistic way in which externally generated volatility of demand can be managed. In either case, the marketing, customer services and IT departments will have to remain in constant contact, which can only benefit the organisation in the longer term.

Customisation is the key differentiator

How can an e-Brand gain a competitive advantage, given that physical retail outlets and online presences are likely to offer the same product?

The answer lies partly in customisation – the adding of value to the customer's overall online experience by making it more personalised and directly relevant. This, in turn, will serve to segment the customer bases into those who prefer to obtain the base product from a retail outlet and others who wish to benefit from the customised version. Even if the customisation is available at the retail outlet, the time delay and incremental cost may not make it a feasible proposition for the customer.

Online customisation, on the other hand, need not come at a great cost to either the supplier or the customer, especially if the customer is prepared to use the self-service tools provided to create the customisation.

And the benefits are considerable. Take the example of an online search engine that allows customers to add news, stock quotes and other services to obtain a customised, personalised page. When the customer needs to use an online search engine, the default option would be to visit the customised page rather than another site whose search engine may be more powerful and offer better results.

Offer value throughout the customer interaction life cycle

Customers have different requirements during each phase of their interaction life cycle, and an e-Brand needs to offer different value during each phase.

- *New customer trials* – these are easier to influence than repeat purchases, using special offers, sample trials, etc.
- *Greater share of existing customers* – who can be induced to favour an organisation's products and services over others in the same category, through cross-sells, personalised welcome and customised offers.
- *Repeat purchases by existing customers over their lifetime* – this is where the revenues and profits of an e-Brand are earned and can be achieved through loyalty programmes, priority service and rewards for referrals attracting new customers.

Where could an e-Brand end up?

Consider the 'shooting star' model shown in Figure 3.1, which illustrates the possible outcomes listed in Table 3.1 for brand values over time as they pass through the growth phase.

Fig. 3.1 The 'shooting star' model

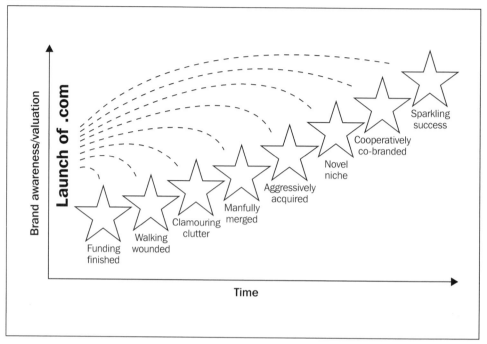

Table 3.1 Possible outcomes for brand values over time

Shooting star type	Typical circumstances
Funding finished	Should funding run out, this star will undoubtedly crash to earth, although there is some benefit to be had from the afterglow of the brand. The value of the brand is, in effect, the database of customers and registrants, the bookmarks on users' computers and the haunting memories of a huge spend on launch advertising.
Walking wounded	This star still glows faintly, surviving on a diet of advertising revenue signed up during its launch phase, and with all running costs having been cut to the bone. This star could have been a winner were it not for a dramatic shift in market sentiment, a new technology or competitors' superior spending firepower. A combination of stubbornness and wounded pride on the part of the founder keeps it glimmering until the inevitable dawn of commercial reality.
Clamouring clutter	This star has joined the clamouring clutter of the billion or so pages on the Internet and is shouting for attention as it attempts to distinguish itself from the pack.
Manfully merged	Although this star could have continued for a while on its own merits, the founder probably took a long-term view. Success was more likely if the business was merged with a competitor in the same market space, a complementary product or service provider or a business with greater financial resources.

Aggressively acquired	This star has a greater intrinsic worth to a third party than to its own founder, given its head start in a specific marketplace and its inability to continue or grow without additional funding. Success is likely to be greater if the acquisition was made to achieve a strategic objective, such as capturing market share before the arrival of a competitor, rather than tactical commercial opportunism.
Novel niche	This star has settled into its own niche, and is content to be recognised only by businesses within whose orbit it has chosen to operate. To retain its success, it will probably engage in vertical integration, even if that involves acquiring real-world components to complement its online offering.
Cooperatively co-branded	This star is a recognised commercial entity in its own right but has chosen to shine even brighter by engaging in co-branding or an alliance with another complementary star that helps it integrate either horizontally or vertically.
Sparkling success	This star has made it through all the trials and tribulations. Its success factors probably include being in the right market space at the right time, a sound business model, professional financial controls, creative yet cost-effective marketing, and a healthy dose of luck.

EXTENDING THE BRAND

An offline brand is probably one of the most powerful items in the corporate arsenal. However, in the rush to grow online, it is increasingly likely to be destroyed by what is supposed to be a positive development – the brand extension or brand leverage (see Table 3.2).

Table 3.2 Range of brand leverage in the real world

Type of leverage	Typical categorisation
Extension	New product in the same segment or category
Expansion	New customer or product segment
Co-brand	Association with a leader in a new segment
New brand	For a new or unrelated business model
Unbranded	For generic association with the product or service (e.g. 1-800-COLLECT for collect calls in the USA, where the telecommunications company behind the service is unbranded)

Brand extension can result in many benefits:

- It can allow the product or service offering to move into a new product class.
- It can increase revenue for the organisation.
- It permits entry into new markets with a reduced marketing spend, given existing customer recognition.
- It prevents competitive entrants from gaining a large market share.
- It uses existing distribution channels to their fullest extent, thereby reducing the overall cost per sale.
- It can refresh the core brand – and generate valuable press coverage.

However, if executed poorly, the negative consequences could reduce the equity of the core brand dramatically. This may happen if:

- each extension has its own positioning and, in the rush to market, some may work against the values of the core brand;
- the image of the core values and benefits of using the brand become blurred in the minds of customers;
- the extended product or service line develops faults or a poor reputation.

So, how can a brand extension be undertaken with minimum risk to the core brand and with the possibility of maximum gain? Unfortunately, there are no hard and fast rules. However, if some essentials are in place, the extension is more likely to be successful:

- There should be a clear link between the original product or service and the extension. The link must be understandable and capable of instant rationalisation in the mind of an existing customer.
- Equally, there should be a clear fit between the core values and those of the brand extension. For example, a car brand built on the core value of safety would be likely to suffer if it extended into manufacturing equipment for high-risk sports.
- A competitive advantage must be created for either the original brand or the extension, or preferably both. This advantage could be derived, for example, from a cross-sell from the core to the extension.

e-Brand historical development

e-Brands have evolved over time – beginning life as simple electronic brochures and developing into highly complex transactional tools. Brand extensions from real-world businesses will, therefore, vary depending upon which stage of development an e-Brand has reached.

Table 3.3 illustrates typical stages in the historical development of e-Brands and their most likely manifestations. Organisations do not have to pass through each stage before progressing to the next, and should enter the development cycle at the point best suited to their specific requirements.

Table 3.3 Typical stages in the historical development of e-Brands and their manifestations

e-Brand development stage	Typical manifestation
Static publishing	Also known as brochureware, at this stage an e-Brand represents nothing more than an electronic version of the corporate annual report and an e-mail link to the webmaster.
Marketing information	This stage saw the first attempts at obtaining a commercial advantage from the Internet, with the online equivalent of printed marketing literature beginning to appear.
Sales information	By now, contact details started to appear, with a bit more information about the products or services available. The sale, however, still had to take place offline, either in the store or by phone or fax.
Self-service	The first glimmers of usefulness appeared here with customers able to help themselves to some information, for example view their statements online.
Transaction processing	This is where the online world really began to blossom, with customers able to interact and transact with equivalent or greater ease than the offline world.
Customisation	At this stage, familiarity with a particular organisation's online presence had grown to such an extent that online customers felt able to customise the site (and the e-Brand) to their preferred operation, behaviour and colour.
Stand-alone subsidiary	When the real-world core brand was extended to a stand-alone subsidiary, the value lay in the subliminal reassurance provided to visitors. In essence, the stand-alone subsidiary borrowed the credibility of the parent.
Web 'pure play'	Attempting to extend a real-world brand to a Web 'pure play' that is unrelated to current business operations is probably one stretch too far.

Table 3.4 illustrates the likely outcomes shown in Figure 3.2 when a real-world business extends its brand into the online world and suggests some typical manifestations of such extensions in the minds of customers.

Table 3.4 Possible brand leverage outcomes and their typical manifestations

Outcome	Typical manifestation
No-win-no-lose	'Hmm, interesting', and pushed to the back of the mind as it does not impact on the relationship with the brand – either positively or negatively.
Only leverage benefits	'Good, now I can get everything I need online', with the often unstated comfort factor – the online presence is backed by the strength of the real-world parent company.
Confusion	'Why is my bank offering me information on lawn mowers?' Possibly because they expect to provide the finance at the point of sale, but this has not been made clear, leading to confusion as to what the brand now represents.
Mutual benefit	'Great – I can study the technical specifications online, visit the showroom for a demonstration, order and have them deliver it. And there's always the call centre if I need after-sales service.' Under this scenario, both offline and online worlds are working with – not against – each other.
Disaster	'Not only did my bank offer me information on lawn mowers last week, they're now offering me reviews of the latest Hollywood movies. Looks like they've lost the Internet plot completely. It's time to move my account to a "real" bank!'

Fig. 3.2 Possible brand leverage outcomes

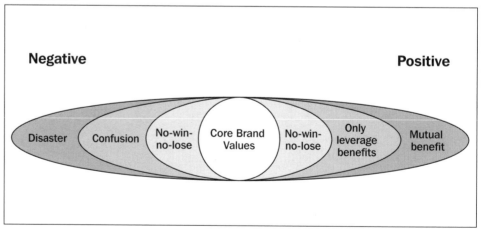

MARKETING – ONLINE AND OFFLINE

Marketing will generate the bulk of the traffic, revenue and profits that will become the equity in an e-Brand. However, the rules of the game have changed considerably with the arrival of online media, and understanding both online marketing and the online customer is vital to success.

The biggest secret is that there are no secrets

The biggest secret in marketing is that there are no secrets. That's because if a marketing campaign of any kind is successful, it will be repeated several times and be impossible to miss. If it fails, it's unlikely to surface a second time. It really is that simple.

Now that the secret's out, how can it be put to good use? As a first step, try to understand the components that comprise a marketing campaign that a competitor has clearly been running for some time. This exercise – a sort of deconstruction – should focus on the individual components such as the offer, the creative execution, the media used and the audience targeted.

Deconstructing campaigns that only had a short shelf life is an equally useful exercise, as it helps highlight the contrast between what works and what doesn't.

It might also be possible to hijack a competitor's successful campaign. Suppose they make a discounted offer to attract new business, with normal terms to apply after 30 days. Towards the 30th day, it might be worth running a similar campaign that is pitched at a rate between the competitor's discounted offer and their normal terms.

Their customers should be attracted to the new deal for two reasons. First, they are already familiar with the campaign, having been educated as to its benefits by your competitor. Second, the new terms they are being offered, while still not as attractive as the competitor's discounted rates, are still better than the normal rates they are about to pay.

Peeling the online marketing onion

Table 3.5 explains some of the typical barriers to online marketing success, with typical reactions from customers or prospects.

Arriving at the goal – a base of loyal, profitable advocates of the online presence – is a bit like peeling an onion. As each layer comes away, a new set of challenges emerges – each strong enough to make a grown man cry.

That's because in the online world – where customers decide which sites they will visit – the failure of the initial interaction could result in the online presence never being revisited – a permanent loss of profits to the e-Brand.

Table 3.5 Barriers to online marketing success

Marketing success barrier	Typical prospect or customer reaction
Inaccurately targeted prospects	'This isn't relevant to me.'
Right prospects, but unaware of online presence	'I didn't know you existed.'
Aware of presence, but unaware of service	'I knew you existed, but I didn't know you offered that service.'
Aware of service, but not evaluated	'I knew about your service, but I didn't include it in my shortlist of suppliers or look into the details.'
Wanted to evaluate, but unable to	'I wanted to evaluate your service, but couldn't find any relevant information on your online presence.'
Evaluated, but not purchased	'I looked at what you had to offer, but decided against buying it.'
Purchased, but not used	'I bought it, but never used it.'
Used, but not frequently	'I used it just a couple of times, but never got the hang of it.'
Frequently used, but let down by service	'I can't get through to customer service, and even if I do, they know less about the product and service than I do.'
Satisfied, but not referred	'It's OK, I suppose, but not something I would feel comfortable about recommending to others.'

Inform, don't sell

Informing or educating customers will, in the long run, generate greater e-Brand loyalty than a price reduction. Competitors can always match – or better – the reduced price offered to customers, but will find it harder to replicate the knowledge you choose to share with your customers.

Best of all, it keeps customers loyal, because it involves earning – not buying – their loyalty. The one-off cost of providing the knowledge is also likely to be less than the price discount, which customers will expect to be repeated. The result – greater profitability over the longer term.

Customers are likely to become increasingly resistant to sales pitches as:

■ they enjoy the luxury of choice – and know they can probably obtain a greater price discount elsewhere;

- they become more cynical – and demand proof of the exaggerated claims and testimonials used to support old-style selling;
- they have access to editorial information – both from independent sources and from other users of the product – which carries more weight than any price discount, especially for products and services related to personal finance, health and children's needs.

Use the magic word – free

Yes, the word 'free' still draws customers like moths to a flame. But there is a greater imperative for using the word 'free' in online marketing compared with the real world. Customers are so accustomed to receiving things free on the Internet that charging for products or services – especially those involving digital content exclusively – is difficult at the best of times.

Give-aways do not have to be expensive to the organisation. While the competition may focus on contests and sweepstakes, it may be worth capturing the moral high ground by offering some editorial content in the give-away. To add to the perceived value of the give-away, and build a database of prospects, the editorial content could have a price attached to it, which is waived if the prospect provides their contact details.

Give-aways also work for intra-site cross-sells and up-sells. Once the customer has made an initial purchase, a give-away leads to another part of the site, which offers a related product or service and increases the total sales generated from the site. It also has the hidden benefit of drawing the depth of the online offering to the customer's attention, and often the incidental page visited carries greater value to the customer than the initial point of entry.

You can't trade a known loss for an unknown gain

That sums up the problem for sites requiring a visitor or prospect to register before they will allow access to information.

Essentially, the deal involves asking for personal details and possibly the completion of a questionnaire – a known loss of privacy and time for the visitor. In return, it offers access to information normally available only to registrants – an unknown gain as, at the time of completing the registration form, the quality and value of the information is not known. Hardly surprising that several visitors leave the site without registering, never to return or experience the benefits the online presence may have brought them.

There are some alternatives that can help get around this thorny issue:

- Make the unknown gain a substantial one. This uses the underlying principle behind lotteries – where a known loss, in the form of the initial investment, is minuscule compared with the potential payout.

- Offer free samples. Once these are studied and found to be satisfactory, there should be no issue with registration on a subsequent visit. Ensure that the samples are truly representative of the rest of the content on the site, or the registrant will feel cheated and engage in e-Brand assassination.

- Obtain the prospect's information in stages. Offer some free samples initially. Then a couple more in exchange for an e-mail address. Then a couple more in exchange for the completion of a questionnaire – and so on.

ONLINE MARKETING CHANNELS

An understanding of the operation and pitfalls of the major online marketing channels is essential to building an e-Brand. Not only do these channels vary materially from their real-world counterparts – assuming they have any – they can also result in some unintended consequences if executed poorly.

Effective tactical execution also results in considerable savings in the marketing budget and forms part of the 'uplift' that results from a series of intelligently integrated campaigns in both the offline and online worlds.

As mentioned earlier in this Executive Briefing, an online presence is passive, and has to wait for prospects to visit. As a result, most of the strategies outlined below are designed to drive traffic to the online presence, while some also assist with encouraging visitors to remain and become familiar with the e-Brand and its operation.

Particular emphasis is paid to three channel strategies that have the potential to generate a far greater upside compared with their cost – these are, specifically, broadcast e-mails, optimising search engines and building affiliate programmes.

Custom domain name

The custom domain name is the best possible start you can give your e-Brand. In essence, it means that your online presence can be found intuitively. For example, someone looking for IBM would not have to visit a search engine to locate the site – they would expect to find it at ibm.com

If an organisation's custom domain name has already been taken, alternative solutions can be found in the earlier section entitled 'But what if the preferred name has already been taken?' on p. 20.

Banner advertisements

Banner advertisements have been one of the staples of online marketing. It is claimed that a single exposure can generate increases in e-Brand awareness and communicate the virtues of using the product or service. By inviting viewers to click the banner advertisement, the first intent – of interest if not purchase – is also registered.

Banner advertisements appear in various shapes and sizes, and a de facto standard exists. The relevant measurements are contained in Table 3.6.

Table 3.6 Banner size and type

Banner size (pixels)	Type
468 × 60	Full banner
392 × 72	Full banner/vertical navigation bar
234 × 60	Half banner
125 × 125	Square button
120 × 90	Button #1
120 × 60	Button #2
88 × 31	Micro button
120 × 240	Vertical banner

Why click-through rates are falling

One of the traditional measures of response is the click-through, when a site visitor clicks on a banner advertisement or a link on one site and is transported to that of the advertiser or link partner.

Click-through rates, traditionally measured as percentages, are calculated by taking the number of click-throughs, divided by the number of impressions (or times the advertisement was seen) and multiplied by 100. So, for example, 20 click-throughs over 1,000 impressions would equate a 2 per cent click-through rate.

The number of click-throughs has been falling for a while and is likely to decline further. It is worth recognising the reasons, as they are equally likely to apply to other Internet marketing strategies:

- The novelty has worn off – except at the start of their Internet experience, people no longer go online to explore for the fun of it.
- Specific searches – the requirement for a specific piece of news or information means that anything that does not lead to the result in the shortest possible time is likely to be ignored, no matter how tempting it might appear.

■ Banner bad behaviour – often, clicking a banner leads to a hung screen, a visit to an inappropriate site, or nowhere at all. These bad experiences have made online users more wary of banners and, by inference, click-throughs.

Links

Links allow users of an online presence to be transferred from that site to the one indicated by the link. The link can be paid for or it can be 'exchanged' with another site (also known as a reciprocal link) without charge, or perhaps a combination of the two.

Links are likely to be more successful if the site on which they appear:

■ provides content similar or related to the site to be linked;

■ places them in a prominent position;

■ promotes them actively, e.g. by recommendation;

■ places them on one or more relevant locations within the site.

Outward facing links may require the user to leave the organisation's online presence, with no guarantee they will return. Where appropriate, possible and legal, outward facing links should launch in a new window within the existing site.

Also, webmasters have been known to place their personal favourite links on the site of their employer, without prior approval. If these are inappropriate, they effectively damage the e-Brand, as they are deemed to have the tacit endorsement of the organisation on whose site they appear.

E-mail

E-mail has been described as the 'killer app' of the Internet and is still its most widely used facet.

Broadcast e-mail represents one of the most cost-effective channels for communication, as it costs a fraction of the investment in, say, a direct mail package, and can be sent to millions of people within a relatively short period.

But it has to be used with care as e-Brand damage can be caused by the following:

■ *Spamming* – the sending of indiscriminate e-mail – or even the perception of spamming. In reality, customers forget whether or not they 'opted in' to receive e-mail news and updates for an organisation. This makes it difficult for them to identify who is e-mailing them without their permission, allowing an organisation to be accused of spamming even when it is not guilty. To reduce this risk, clearly state at the top of each communication that the recipient is receiving this only because they have previously registered and allow them an opportunity to unsubscribe at any time.

- *Frequency of e-mail contact that is inconsistent with the product or service being offered* – e.g. for a seasonal product or service, such as gardening, a quarterly e-mail would be justified.

- *Inappropriateness of content* – e-mail communications should be mostly editorial with a sprinkling of promotional offers, not the other way round.

- *Failing to specify source* – most e-mail systems do not show the full subject line or the full e-mail address of the sender – just the first few characters. If both of these do not contain the source of the e-mail, i.e. an organisation's name, they could be mistaken for virus carriers and deleted without being opened.

- *Failing to understand technology* – this can take the form of, among other problems, the following:

  - E-mail systems, especially those drawing data from a live database, have been known to send the same message more than once to a recipient, causing considerable annoyance.

  - Hyperlinks included within the e-mail cannot be opened directly, often due to the ISP or e-mail program used by the recipient. But this is assumed to be due to the technical incompetence of the sender, unless there is an alternative that suggests users 'cut and paste' the hyperlink into the address line of the browser.

  - Recipients also have the habit of responding to broadcast e-mails, even though they should not. This results in them receiving an 'undeliverable' message, again creating the impression of organisational technical incompetence.

  - If recipient e-mails are returned as 'undeliverable', this is sometimes not fed back to the database for cleaning, resulting in inaccuracies growing over time.

- *Creativity* – with response rates from broadcast e-mails to opt-in lists decreasing, organisations might be tempted to get 'creative' in their attempts to get recipients to open the e-mail. Several variations on the theme exist, but none of the following should ever be implemented as they are also the favoured tools of fraudsters:

  - False timeline – URGENT, OPEN NOW! – even though there is no genuine need to do so.

  - False name – 'Dear Fred' to someone not called Fred, hoping that curiosity will encourage them to open and read the message.

  - False courtesy – 'Hope you don't mind this message, but I thought you'd like to know about...'

- False subject line – 'Hot secrets inside' – while the text in the body of the e-mail talks about the move to a new corporate headquarters.
- False associations – 'News from the UN' – pretending to be more closely associated with a prestigious organisation or charity than is actually the case.

e-Zines

The ability to distribute corporate literature online, at relatively minimal cost, has contributed to the phenomenal growth of electronic magazines, commonly referred to as e-Zines.

However, the ease of distribution often blinds organisations to other economic and logistical realities that apply to such endeavours in both the offline and online worlds. These include the need for:

- relevant and timely content;
- professional editing and design;
- clearance of compliance and regulatory issues, where appropriate.

Absence of any of the above, on a regular basis, probably explains why a substantial number of corporate e-Zines never make it past issue number 1.

e-Branding implications for e-Zines are the same as those for any printed corporate material – editorial value, accuracy, regularity of circulation and consistency with the brand positioning. However, there are a number of online-specific nuances worth bearing in mind, which could end up tarnishing the e-Brand.

- e-Zines tend to be categorised alongside e-mail – immediate and instinctive – within the corporate mindset. As a result, they are sometimes despatched at the last minute without the appropriate proofreading, often with embarrassing results. The simple expedient of sending out a couple of copies to favoured customers – who can point out potential misinterpretations – is often ignored.
- The cheapness of online media – compared with their real-world equivalents – also proves to be a temptation too great to resist for online marketers. e-Zines are often set up with the noblest of intentions, but metamorphose into promotional pieces with advertising posing as editorial or increasing ratios of advertising to genuine editorial.
- Distribution issues have been covered above in the section on 'e-mail' but include multiple copies being sent to the same person, poorly directed response mechanisms and so on.
- The pace of change in the online world means that decisions are often made in 'stop–start–stop' mode. A decision to start an e-Zine today, with great fanfare

and exaggerated promises, often looks foolish when the second issue never appears, say because of the need to reduce the cash burn.

All of these tend to tarnish the e-Brand.

A simple checklist can help determine whether an e-Zine should ever be launched. Answering 'yes' to all of the questions below would increase the chances of successfully launching an e-Zine that adds to the e-Brand value.

- Will it add value to the organisation's marketing and branding efforts?

- Will it add value to customers – by reducing the frequency of other smaller communications, providing editorial and news, etc.? Have customers been consulted on their views as to the need for an e-Zine?

- Is there an executive-level sponsor for the project? Is he or she prepared to fund the project and ensure editorial integrity?

- Has a budget – that will not be revoked – been agreed for this project for at least two years?

- Have suppliers – in the form of editors, designers and e-mail distribution agencies – been identified?

- Is there a guaranteed supply of quality editorial and content? Have clear themes been identified?

- Has IT agreed to provide a clean and up-to-date list prior to each distribution run?

- Are the legal, compliance, privacy and data protection personnel within the organisation in agreement with the concept and prepared to set aside time to pre-clear each issue?

Press releases

Appearing as a newsworthy item in print, or on respected online news and information sites, can drive traffic to the online presence. The quality of this traffic is likely to be better than that generated by advertising, because it is unlikely to contain short-term offer seekers. Converting these visitors into customers, therefore, not only generates revenue but also builds reputation.

However, crafting and issuing press releases can be a considerable waste of time if not handled effectively. Some tactics that are likely to increase the chances of success include the following:

- Don't give journalists the story – point them in the right direction and make all relevant facts available, when they ask for them.

- When pitching a story, explain the reason for communicating with them, the key idea in a couple of sentences and why the story works for their publication.

- Ensure the story has not passed its 'sell by' date. Stories issued before their due date can be embargoed until the appropriate time.

- Keep the story within the boundaries of reality – edit out all exaggeration. The most respected online sites have a person-to-person writing style, and their writers take considerable delight in deflating the pomposity of press releases.

- Keep the word count down – 300 words is great for the initial attention-grabbing phase. Some online sites will edit this down further and include a hyperlink for site visitors who need more information.

- Make sure to include the address of the online presence – especially to the specific pages referred to in the press release, if appropriate.

- Set up an electronic press area if one does not exist already. This is a resource for journalists and should include relevant photographs in common digital formats such as gif or jpeg, and text in common formats such as .doc, .txt, .rtf and .pdf which can be viewed in its original layout by tools such as Adobe® Acrobat Reader.

- Respond quickly when contacted. Journalists have deadlines to meet and will be grateful to anyone who helps them.

- Recognise that both parties need each other. Journalists need an organisation's knowledge base and news while the organisation needs the exposure.

- Keep in touch and build relationships. The value of friendly press contacts is that it minimises the pain during periods of unfavourable coverage by others.

- Keep a damage limitation plan ready, and rehearse it regularly. It will be needed one day – when there is a major technology failure or for circumstances beyond the organisation's control.

Newsgroups, electronic mailing lists, chat rooms and bulletin boards

Both newsgroups and subscriber-driven electronic mailing lists have one thing in common – they contain groups of people who share a common interest and have chosen to join.

The irritation and anger of the self-selected users of these services is understandable when they find themselves at the receiving end of electronic promotional material, often unrelated to their area of interest. The result is 'flaming' of the sender, and all that will remain from such a transgression are the ashes of the e-Brand.

Access to these valuable groups can be obtained by selective and sensitive contribution to the daily discussions, some of which can include discreet references to the organisation. If the contribution is intelligent and valuable, members will seek more information on the sender. If the sender just happens to have a signature file at the bottom of the posting, containing name, e-mail address and the hyperlinked web address of the organisation, this will facilitate access to the site by group members.

All of the above equally apply to chat rooms, where real-time conversations can be had with people who share a common interest, or bulletin boards, where people post messages seeking or offering comment. The chat room moderator reserves the right to bar inappropriate content, which could include promotional messages in what is essentially an information and advice-sharing medium.

Having someone within the organisation monitor and contribute to all relevant newsgroups, electronic mailing lists, chat rooms and bulletin boards may seem like a waste of time and money. However, this form of 'lurking' not only serves to drive quality traffic to the site, it also provides advance warning of online rumours which can be squashed before they become 'facts' simply because of repetition.

Sponsorship

Sponsorships are increasing in popularity on the Internet and occur when an organisation pays to appear – in a non-sales context – on another organisation's site. The sponsor's presence is indicated by a banner, button or statement supporting a particular event or cause, and is usually positioned on a relevant portion of the site and included within the e-Zine.

Tags on all online and offline material

Once the brand guidelines are in place, ensure that all online and offline material – whether promotional or not – contains the organisation's website address and an e-mail address. Inbound e-mail must be examined daily and routed to the most relevant person within the organisation for immediate response.

This is not intended to suggest the indiscriminate application of ugly stickers to anything and everything that moves. Instead, be watchful so as not to let opportunities for appropriate awareness slip by.

Offline media particularly suited to this approach include letterheads, envelopes, invoices, business cards and all promotional material such as direct mail.

Online, this can be best deployed via a signature file (sig.file). When attached to the end of every outbound e-mail, this block of text not only identifies the sender (name, address, job title) but also provides contact details, such as phone, fax and e-mail address.

The key is to include a very short marketing message and the web address or uniform resource locator (URL) of the organisation. Clicking on the hyperlinked URL will take the recipient of the e-mail directly to the organisation's online presence, and is a subtle – yet highly effective – mechanism for promoting the business, even in newsgroups. Should the e-mail be forwarded by the recipient to a third party for business reasons, another set of eyes will see the promotional material – at no cost to the organisation.

Building an online reputation

With a billion or more pages on the Web, it is reasonable to assume that online presences offering authoritative editorial content are likely to triumph over those specialising in cheap offers and marketing hyperbole.

While building an online reputation takes time, the rewards can be equally long lasting. The following strategies can help build a reputation:

- Infiltrate all relevant industry associations at the earliest stage of their development – offering not just money, but also time from senior executives. This allows the organisation to influence the growth and development of the association in a mutually beneficial manner. Should the association become a self-regulatory or licensing authority over time, the organisation will be well placed, not only as the originator of high standards, but also to exclude competitors who might bring the industry into disrepute. Irrespective of the management involvement, the organisation should compete keenly for all relevant industry awards, as these build credibility and reputation.

- Contribute editorial to industry publications. Not only does this establish an organisation – and some of its key executive team – as experts in their area, it is effectively free exposure for the organisation's e-Brand and URL. The volume of online traffic originating from such published efforts may not be large, but the quality of the visitors, and their propensity to convert into customers, should be far better than advertising-led traffic. The editorial can also be recycled. Other complementary sites could be offered the material provided they include a hyperlink to the organisation's site and present the appropriate copyright notices in a prominent manner.

- Lead forum discussions – serving as a guest expert within an online forum is another excellent vehicle for building credibility and visibility with a receptive and highly targeted audience. Online agencies which set up forums with high-traffic sites could be engaged to manage the logistics. If the performance of the executive clearly demonstrates an understanding of the subject matter, invitations to speak to the real-world press will certainly follow.

Personalisation and customisation

One of the greatest strengths of the online world is the ability to personalise the messages to prospects and customise the online presence to regular users. This can take several forms, including:

- Personalised 'welcome back' messages, based on cookies placed on the users' computers.

- Collaborative filtering – presenting recommendations for future purchases based on information collated on the purchases made by other like-minded customers.

- Offering interactive tools, e.g. personal finance calculators, that are relevant to the products and services offered by the online presence, and that keep users longer, during which time they may choose to explore previously unvisited areas and build greater familiarity with the e-Brand.

- Pre-completing forms, based on information provided earlier, to allow customers direct access to new services without having to re-submit data provided earlier. Instead, they should be offered the opportunity to update or edit the data.

- Inviting completion of questionnaires, which suggest the users' views are important, possibly backed by a non-cash reward. This continuous feedback loop, where users are thanked and pointed to an area of the site which has been amended following their comments, is a powerful e-Brand building tool.

However, the misuse of personalisation techniques could backfire on the e-Brand, given its Orwellian connotations, and is discussed in detail in Chapter 4 on protecting your e-Brand.

Search engine and directory optimisation

The majority of successful Internet sites get a substantial amount of their daily traffic of new visitors from popular search engines and directories.

Search engines mostly use robots (also known as spiders or webcrawlers) to visit as many sites as possible, analyse them and index their findings. Directories (the most famous of which is probably Yahoo!) rely on manual submissions by site owners, which are then individually considered by their editors for inclusion and categorisation.

Each search engine or directory has unique requirements. Understanding these increases the chances of the site being accurately categorised and ranked within the first 10 results of any search using a related or relevant keyword.

Broadly speaking, the top-ranking pages in the search results are the home pages of websites, where the domain name contains the keywords being searched.

The following guidance should increase search engine results visibility and is based on managing the process and information used by search engines to categorise and position the site:

- *Clear layout* – on each page of the site allows search engine robots to locate, identify and classify the site. To get this process started, it may be necessary to submit the site for consideration, either manually on a case-by-case basis, or via a multiple submission site, which is less effective.

- *Metatags* – are carefully selected keywords and descriptions of the functionality of the site, which are stored on the site but are not visible to visitors or users. Abuse of metatags – such as repeating the same word several times or including inappropriate words with the objective of diverting traffic – has led major search engines to blacklist sites that overuse this feature.

- *Content* – articles, tutorials and other materials related to the site increase the chances of being visited and indexed by search engines, resulting in greater visibility.

- *Multiple doorways* – are web pages expressly built for the sole purpose of increasing search engine rankings. They may be critical for websites that use dynamically generated pages – where the information is only called up from a database when requested – as search engine robots have nothing to index when they arrive. However, search engines frown on this practice and others such as cloaking (see Chapter 4, p. 100) on the basis that visitors see a different page to that shown to the search engine robot and this compromises the integrity of the search.

- *Firewalls and password activation* – sites located behind secure corporate firewalls or which are password-activated will also be penalised in the rankings as they restrict or disallow access to search engine robots. In essence, a trade-off is being made between obtaining user information prior to allowing access to a site and a lower ranking on search engine results.

Optimising the results on popular search engines is a skilled task and expert assistance should be sought, as each search engine's submission requirements are unique. Payment could be based on results, which may take several weeks to materialise, depending upon the volume of voluntary submissions to search engine robots or the workload of directory editors.

Affiliate programmes

The concept behind affiliate programmes is relatively simple and the closest real-world equivalent would be the 'commission only' salesperson.

Online, the process generally works as follows:

- A site (call it 'X') – through its owner or webmaster – joins the affiliate programme of another site (call it 'Y'). Registration is usually done online through a discrete part of the site.

- A web visitor arrives at X.

- Clicking the relevant banner or link directs them to Y.

- A purchase is made at Y.

- Y pays X a commission – on a predetermined scale and at agreed dates.

Affiliate programmes have their pros and cons:

- They are successful as they use several different organisations and personal sites to sell to their visitors. The selling sites are effectively converting their credibility with visitors into revenue by recommending they visit the affiliate and make a purchase there. A poor experience will, however, damage the relationship between the referring party and their customer.

- Affiliates may use innovative techniques to induce sales, as they are not constrained by the technical or cultural constraints of the organisation running the affiliate programme. Counterbalancing that is the risk that the affiliate may make unapproved, unsubstantiated or exaggerated claims to induce the sale – but the customer blames the site at which the sale is actually consummated.

- Although affiliate programmes do not consume the volumes of cash associated with high-profile advertising campaigns, they do require investment and maintenance. They also do not generate instant results, taking up to a year to generate their first worthwhile revenue contributions.

- Choosing affiliate partners is as important as choosing friends and business partners in the real world. Find the right ones, and there can be a long-standing, mutually beneficial relationship. Get one wrong and the time, energy and expense needed to dissolve the relationship, and protect the e-Brand, is considerable.

With affiliate programmes delivering a significant proportion of retail sales (as in the case of Amazon.com), an organisation would have to consider establishing one as an economic necessity. The following checklist should help increase the chances of success in establishing – and maintaining – an affiliate programme.

- *Appoint an affiliate champion.* This person, who should be a senior executive within the organisation, is responsible for the success of the programme. This includes establishing clear rules for the operation of the programme, marketing, vetting affiliates, processing the sales, and providing comprehensive ongoing support to the affiliates.

- *Let everyone know the affiliate programme exists.* This extends beyond the obvious option of hyperlinking to the affiliate programme portion of the site via the home page and having a clear and simple online application process. It includes registering the affiliate programme with specialist directories (such as Refer-it) and deploying as many online marketing tactics as possible. The corporate e-Zine and e-mail signature files are obvious candidates, along with corporate stationery.

- *Make the programme attractive for the affiliates.* Whether it is a per-transaction fee, a commission on sales or even a payment per click-through, if the results aren't economically attractive for the affiliate they are unlikely to enrol. If profit margins are slim, an affiliate programme may not be the correct marketing channel and should not be commenced.

- *Make the terms crystal clear.* This refers not only to payment terms, but also the conditions under which enrolment can be terminated, e.g. for breach of security, data protection, privacy, unsubstantiated sales claims, etc. A legally binding agreement won't eliminate disputes, but it will allow for speedier resolution.

- *Set up clear FAQs.* Think of affiliates as customers who are likely to have questions about the programme. Have these been answered clearly in the FAQs (frequently asked questions)? Have the FAQs been updated regularly?

- *Allow affiliates to track their success online.* By providing associates with password-protected access to their sales results, not only is pressure on support staff eased, but associates can also keep a running tab on their likely income, after allowing for any customer returns and refunds.

- *Be reasonable.* When market conditions get difficult, there is a tendency to extract greater value from the affiliates. This may extend to creating unreasonable contracts such as multi-year terms, prohibition on dealing with the programme's competitors, etc. Not only will this discourage potential affiliates, it will simply encourage existing affiliates to cheat, as the investment in ensuring compliance is disproportionate to the revenue saved.

There is only one way to ensure a successful affiliate programme – treat them as well as favoured customers, and they will repay the investment with steadily increasing sales.

SPECIALIST ONLINE MARKETING STRATEGIES

Customers are loyal – to anyone with a special offer

Loyalty programmes online generally face the same advantages and pitfalls as their offline counterparts – with some subtle distinctions.

- *Limited online attention span* – as this is usually very limited, any complex set of rules and regulations is unlikely to be read or acted upon. Simplicity is key for online loyalty programmes.

- *Online savings should be shared* – as online loyalty programmes are likely to make processing savings, e.g. by not issuing monthly paper statements, these savings should be shared with programme participants, and this fact should be clearly communicated.

- *Issue resolution* – if there is unlikely to be any human involvement in running the online loyalty programme, even in the event of difficulties, the alternatives (such as FAQs) should be comprehensive and easy to understand.

- *Realise value in the offline world* – the savings, points, etc. earned in the online loyalty programme should be capable of conversion into tangible physical items in the offline world, if that is what the participant chooses. It is easy to see why fewer redemption options – for example, points are only redeemable against digital content from the programme site – make the programme less successful.

For an organisation's loyalty programme to retain its members in the face of competitive offers, it has to offer practical, measurable value for being loyal – customised offers, privileged information, preferential service, etc. – consistently across all the touch-points the customer is likely to come across.

Having a reliable, operational, secure and easily navigable online presence is taken as read.

At last – three friendly viruses

Viral marketing is, broadly speaking, any technique that induces a website or user to carry a marketing message to another website or user, creating potentially exponential growth in the visibility and effect of the message.

There are three categories of viruses that can be used to carry the e-Brand message to all corners of the globe. If, when and how they should be used is at the discretion of the organisation, but their modus operandi is explained below.

Passive

This form of virus does not require any action from the carrier and is essentially dormant. Upon arrival, however, it can be activated by the recipient, who then effectively becomes another carrier.

For example, a leading web-based e-mail service attaches a one-line message to every outbound e-mail it sends on behalf of its customers. Customers have to do nothing – and are unable to object as they use the service free of charge. The recipient may click the hyperlink, visit the site, and open a free web-based e-mail account. The original recipient now becomes another carrier of the virus.

Participative

This strain of the virus requires the recipient to participate in a more active manner. The sender (called X) requires the recipient (called Y) to take some action in order to conclude the transaction or obtain a benefit.

For example, X decides to use the service of a web-based greeting card company. After designing the card, X decides not to e-mail it directly to Y, as the size of the graphics may require Y to spend considerable time downloading the file. Instead X uses a form on the site to e-mail Y advising of the availability of the card. Y has to go to the site, using the hyperlink provided in the e-mail, to retrieve the card and enjoy the message. X has now forced Y to visit the site. What's more, the next time Y needs the services of an electronic greeting card site, Y is likely to return to the site introduced by X.

Evangelical

This is the most virulent strain of the virus (to date) and involves X becoming an evangelist for the site in order to convince Y to use it.

For example, X wishes to use a particular chat program to communicate with Y. Unfortunately, Y is not particularly technologically literate and finds the prospect of downloading and installing the software a daunting one. X will have to go to considerable lengths – such as visiting Y's home, logging on to the site, installing the program and educating Y in its operation. Once they become regular users, both X and Y are likely to become evangelists for the site as they attempt to extend its usage to their friends.

Stunt marketing

This strategy is usually deployed in the real world when desperate times call for desperate measures. In the online world, however, it seems to be more commonplace, probably in response to the 'noise' level from all the promotion campaigns related to the billion or so pages on the Web. This triumph of showmanship over substance manifests itself in several ways – wacky advertising, street theatre, ludicrous claims and near illegal competitions.

Here's the problem. Stunt marketing operates under the misguided assumption that whoever screams loudest wins. While this may be true for the few moments that the screaming is in progress, it cannot be sustained.

Not only will the screaming have driven away potential customers who do not react well to this style of communication, but those it did attract are unlikely to remember the name of the organisation doing the screaming, especially when another organisation arrives offering even louder toys.

Organisations – other than those owning fun, lifestyle brands – considering stunt marketing as a means for promoting their e-Brand should heed this advice – don't!

Lateral thinking might help

Unusual forms of marketing, born from lateral thinking, might yield a better return on the marketing investment.

For example, giving each employee a home PC with Internet access could have multiple advantages. Say, some of them create a personal home page and link it to their employer. Casual visitors might find this loyalty touching and visit the employer's site.

Some employees might visit bulletin boards and defend the organisation if it is being unfairly maligned. Others will speak of the generosity of the employing organisation to friends and family, creating a favourable impression that could result in offline sales. Others might arrange for their employer to support their local recreational group, which then links to the employee's home page, which in turn links to a separate section on the employer's site. And so on, and so forth.

ONLINE CUSTOMERS CAN BE FOUND IN THE STRANGEST PLACES

Profit by association

Rather than having just a single front door – the home page – an organisation's online presence should have multiple entry points into the site.

To do this requires tuning into the mindset of a typical customer – where would such a person look in addition to the obvious? What alternative doorways could they come through if they had the opportunity?

For example, a site marketing table lamps might consider obtaining banner advertisements, links or maybe even a mention on the site of the publisher of an interior decoration magazine, a bookseller, table manufacturers and so on.

Or an appliance manufacturer could set up micro-sites in portals aimed at home furnishings, department store sites and others. Just as in the real world, offering a couple of, say, dishwashers at low rates would encourage the owners of the sites to aggressively promote the manufacturer's brand and micro-site location.

If managed proactively, the site traffic through these doors might, over time, exceed that arriving through the front door.

Avoid paying for new customers

There are a few situations where it is possible to grow an e-Brand without having to pay – in marketing costs – for customer acquisition.

- In the first scenario, the organisation might be providing an alternative for a regulatory requirement, as part of an increasing trend whereby governments subcontract some of their processes to private firms. For example, the renewal of a mandatory licence could be undertaken over the organisation's online presence rather than having to queue in a local government office.

- Another scenario might involve the organisation offering its online presence to the employees of a company. For example, the provider of house cleaning or dry cleaning services for busy employees could be given access to employees via the corporate intranet or extranet in return for discounted rates. The service provider saves on the marketing costs of acquiring those customers and the employer is seen to be providing a value-added service at preferential rates to employees – a win–win situation.

BEWARE!

Out of sight, out of mind

One of the major issues for an e-Brand is that it does not exist when the device on which it is viewed is switched off. That's why it might be worth creating tangible, physical reminders of the e-Brand. Commonly used solutions include mouse-mats, and trinkets that can be affixed to the monitor. The more creative the solution, the better. There is one proviso – it must be consistent with the values and imagery promoted by the e-Brand.

Once online, the browser's bookmark function remains one of the best places to jog a recalcitrant memory.

Tunnel vision

It is often difficult to re-educate existing customers following an extension of the original product or service suite that was in place when they first became a customer. Force of habit means they will continue to use only the original limited functionality and visit another site for what is essentially a competing service. As an example, the perception of Amazon.com as an online bookstore persists, despite it having added countless other product streams.

Tracking regular users' movements throughout the site and greeting them with an announcement of a new service every time they log in might get them to change their behaviour – eventually.

ONLINE MEASUREMENT

Measuring results in the offline world is not just important – it is critical for the success of the e-Brand. Rapidly changing commercial environments will require swift changes in strategies, but the success or failure of these strategies must be known sooner rather than later so as to allow for refinement or abandonment.

Unlike the offline world, the online world allows for the real-time collection, analysis and presentation of data. Wasting this opportunity could cost an e-Brand dearly.

If you don't measure, how do you know what's working?

In the offline world, an oft-quoted comment goes something like this: 'I know half my advertising is wasted, I just don't know which half.' No such observation is possible in the online world, where just about everything is measurable – and near-instantaneously.

The case for measurement is a foolproof one. No measurement = no ability to understand which campaigns are working and which are failing = wasted marketing budget = continued poor targeting and campaign execution = reduced e-Brand valuation.

And unlike the real world, cost cannot be used as an excuse. With minimal expenditure and effort, it is possible to obtain a reasonably accurate picture of the source of visitors, their behaviour while on the site and their purchasing patterns.

Typical marketing management reports would answer the following questions or include the relevant statistics:

- number of unique visitors to the site;
- origin of unique visitors to the site – are they customers or competitors? did they arrive from banner advertising or reciprocal links on other sites?
- which day of the week – and which time during the day – is the site at its busiest?
- number of visits to each page within the site;
- average time spent on each page;
- access time per page;
- error messages when accessing a page;
- number of sales;
- pages visited immediately prior to a sale.

Putting these pieces of the jigsaw together and then attempting to constantly improve the results will optimise the marketing spend and, by inference, the e-Brand. With the ability to test marketing campaigns within hours, and personalise communications 'on-the-fly', the online world is truly an intelligent marketing manager's dream come true.

Designing by analysis

Measurement has other hidden benefits. By identifying behavioural patterns, it allows users to be categorised by these – rather than demographics such as age and gender – which can then be used to make design changes to the site.

For example, there might be material behavioural differences between those who made a purchase on the site and those who didn't. Perhaps they visited a 'user's comments' section immediately prior to making the purchase. Design changes to the site can then be made to encourage potential non-purchasers to visit the 'user's comments' section and help modify their behavioural patterns.

Don't forget external measurements

In days gone by, a brand provided a guide through the range of choices available at retail level. It represented certain quality standards, which served to overcome the absence of comparative data that was unavailable or difficult to obtain.

No longer. The Internet provides ease of access to rich information sources, reducing the 'guiding' role of the brand. And this information is available not just from manufacturers, but from other customers as well.

These can be found at sites ranging from amateurish gripe sites, through to sophisticated opinion sites run by businesses for the sole purpose of advising customers of the views of other customers. Most of these carry a proprietary rating system, and it is important to compare these external results with those generated internally.

Material variances, if any, could be due to various factors – including inaccuracy of measurement on the organisation's internal site to a concerted campaign to tarnish the e-Brand on external opinion sites. In either case, the variance should be investigated and action taken.

Repeat versus new users

Not all measures are created equal. For example, it costs between 5 and 50 times more to acquire a new customer than it does to retain an existing one, depending on which marketing textbook one reads.

Therefore, an existing customer who has become dormant should carry a greater weighting than a first-time visitor when conducting an analysis of site traffic and determining where marketing funding is to be directed.

There are other differences between first-time users and repeat users that affect measurement. For example, a group of experienced users might navigate the site faster because they chose to turn off certain help functionality or even the graphical elements of the site.

This should not justify switching off the functionality across the site. Instead, two standard measures for site usage should be created – one for the experienced users who know precisely where everything is located, and another for first-time visitors.

No, the cookies are not poisoned

Some of the fear surrounding the use of 'cookies' is clearly indicative of a misunderstanding of their role in tracking and securing site visits.

Cookies are identifiers used by an organisation to store information about their site users' interactions with selected areas of their online presence. On subsequent visits, the cookie passes back and forth between the organisation's server and the user's browser, allowing the repeat visitor to be recognised and, in most cases, rewarded with everything ranging from personalised information to special offers.

Increasingly, cookies play a role in identifying site visitors for security reasons, and several web-based service providers will not allow access to their sites if cookies are switched off or deleted. Cookies can be sent to the primary domain which originated them (e.g. xyz.com) or a sub-domain thereof (e.g. new.xyz.com), but not to an entirely different domain (e.g. abc.com).

There is the possibility that some cookie information could be matched against databases of e-mail addresses and physical addresses, should these become known in the course of e-Commerce activities, and then rented or sold to third parties. But, as yet, cookies cannot steal the contents of a hard drive and forward them to the world at large!

What, exactly, are you measuring – and paying for?

The flip side of the measurement coin is payment by results. And these results are measured using terminology that is unique to the online world – but not necessarily consistent across the globe.

Worse still, hiding behind the mind-boggling figures for hits, page views, etc. is a truckload of shortcomings in the measurements and their interpretation.

Table 3.7 is a summary (in increasing order of accuracy) of the leading online measures and their shortcomings. Studying these carefully will allow the exaggerated claims by site owners to be brought down to earth – while making substantial savings in the marketing budget.

Table 3.7 Understanding e-Advertising and e-Marketing measures – and their limitations

Measure	Description	Limitations
Hit or gross exposure	A record in the web server of a file sent to a web browser. Each element of the file – text, graphic, video – registers as a separate 'hit'. Of value to webmasters, who use this as one measure of the server's workload.	Over-counting – if a page containing 5 graphics and 2 applets is sent by the web server, it will be recorded as 8 hits. This is computed by adding 5 graphics, 2 applets and 1 hit for the page itself.
Valid hits	A refinement on the concept of hits – which excludes any error messages, internal requests or computer originated hits (e.g. a spider robot from a search engine).	Over-counting – as above.
Visit/visitor session	A visit is a series of requests from a visitor to an Internet site. The visitor session is deemed to have ended when no request has been made for a predefined period of time known as the 'time-out' period. Attempts have been made to standardise this, with 30 minutes increasingly regarded as the norm. A subsequent request outside the time-out period from the same visitor would be treated as a new visit.	Poor identification – if the same individual makes a page request outside the original 'time-out' period, it is regarded as a second visit. No industry standard – some advertising sales people reduce the 'time-out' period to generate higher visitor session figures for their site. Misleading analytics – some external measurement agencies use sample groups to estimate site visits, rather than analysing actual site server logs, to which the site owners may not provide access. If the sample is unrepresentative, the resulting analytics will be equally unrepresentative of reality.
Page views or gross impressions	This is recorded when a complete HTML page, inclusive of all graphics, text and interactive files, is delivered. This measure indicates the number of times a page was requested – and an advertisement potentially seen on the page. Works on the premise that if	Each frame and frame parent document is counted as an individual page, so viewing a home page might actually be three or more page views. Over-counting – page views are counted irrespective of whether or not advertising was displayed on the page, so over-counting could still be present.

a page was requested, there is an intention to view the content. Only some pages of the site may qualify as advertisable page impressions – pages capable of hosting banner advertisements.

Potential, not actual, viewing – the page might be viewed, but not the advertisement. Similar to a TV which is switched on, with the viewer channel hopping during the advertisements.

If users switch off graphics to increase browsing speed and read content, the number of page views – and potential advertising impressions – might rise, but it is even less likely the advertisements will be viewed.

Changing the server's 'refresh' frequency could instantly change the number of page views, as each refresh would register page views.

| Advertising views or ad views | Number of times an advertising banner is served – and assumed to be seen – by the site visitor. Most web pages have more than one advertisement, so the number of ad views is greater than the equivalent page views.

Payment is on the basis of CPM – cost per mille or cost per thousand impressions. Example – a £20,000 banner campaign with a guaranteed 800,000 impressions would equate to a CPM of £25. Rates vary as to whether the ads are served run-of-site (i.e. anywhere) or if specific selections are required (e.g. geography, time of day, specific site location). | Under-counting – to speed surfing, a web browser would cache (store) recently visited pages on a user's hard disk. If the site is revisited, or the same ad appears on multiple pages simultaneously, the browser will display pages from disk, rather than the site's web server, thereby under-counting the number of ad views. To reduce this possibility, cache-busting software is deployed by servers pushing banner advertisements.

Other non-standard measures include counting a single impression on a co-branded banner as two impressions. Alternatively, an ad for software for kids could be counted twice – once in each category. Understanding the methodology used – and having access to ad server logs – is the only way to ensure the online advertising budget is being fairly spent. |
| Click-through or ad click | This occurs when a visitor physically clicks on an advertisement and is transported to another page | Cost-per-click is another charging mechanism, i.e. £0.20 per click paid by the advertiser to the site owner. However, this can be |

or website, i.e. a tangible response to a banner advertisement.

Click-through rate (CTR) is calculated as the number of clicks divided by the number of ad impressions multiplied by 100 and expressed as a percentage. Example – 15 clicks over 1,000 impressions would equate to a CTR of 1.5%.

abused by the advertiser, by placing an ad that does not call for action, e.g. 'click here now for ...', as the ad will continue to enjoy ad views but no payment will be due to the site owner. The 'ad' may actually be a smaller-sized button, in which case location on the site is all-important if a high CTR is to be achieved. Buttons may be more responsive than banner advertisements, despite their size.

Keyword

This occurs when a 'keyword' such as 'flights' is purchased (e.g. by a travel agent) on a site, usually a search engine. Every time the search query includes the keyword, the banner ad provided by the travel agent will be served and charged at a predetermined rate per display.

Beware – a competitor could choose an organisation's name as the keyword, ensuring that every time it was entered as part of a search query, the advertising banner served above the result (showing the organisation's name) was that of the competitor.

Unique host

An attempt to identify site visitors by their Internet protocol (IP) address – i.e. the computer from which they arrived.
A common advertising measure is unique hosts per month. It should track all unique hosts over a 30-day period to ensure each 'unique' host is counted only once, irrespective of the number of visits during the 30-day period.

Under-counting – in certain situations, e.g. a cyber café, two separate individuals visiting the same site would share the same proxy server IP address and be treated as a single unique host, thereby under-counting the number of users.
Over-counting – again, in a cyber café situation, a person visiting the same site twice with an interval between the two visits could be routed via two different proxy servers owned by the café. Although two unique hosts, it is still the same person.
Some site owners compensate for the under-counting by multiplying their unique host numbers by an arbitrary number, say 3, to arrive at a count for unique users.
Unique hosts per month are often computed by adding together all the daily unique hosts over a

		30-day period regardless of the fact that some of them might have visited on more than one day during that 30-day period, thereby inflating the figures considerably.
Unique user	A distinct individual who visits a website or page within a specified 'time-out' period. Identification is undertaken by user registration or other tracking devices such as cookies.	The same individual visiting the site outside the original 'time-out' period will be counted as two unique users even though it is the same person. Cookies can be intentionally disabled by visitors or disallowed by corporate firewalls making tracking impossible. If the user logs on via a different computer to the one on which the cookie was placed, e.g. a laptop, then a new cookie will be set and counted as a new unique user even though it is the same person.
Registered user	A distinct individual who visits a website, enters personal details and an identification password, and is granted access.	If the individual forgets or loses the password on an information (not transactional) site, they could re-register with a new password. Again, it is the same person, but with two 'registered user' accounts.

Pareto principle still applies

The Pareto principle states that a small number of causes (usually 20 per cent) is responsible for a large percentage of the effects (usually 80 per cent).

It can be broadly applied across every aspect of online measurement. For example, 20 per cent of customers will most probably contribute 80 per cent of profits; 20 per cent of sites on which banner advertisements are served will generate 80 per cent of the traffic to the site – and so on.

If any specific measurements generated by the organisation vary materially from those expected under the Pareto principle they should be re-investigated, first for accuracy, and subsequently to determine whether the lessons learned can be applied to other aspects of marketing or design across the site.

CUSTOMER SERVICE

Being available 365 days a year is great for sales, but what about service?

Being 'live' on the Internet is a great concept for anyone interested in generating revenue. Anyone can make a purchase from the online presence from anywhere in the world, at any time, day or night. The fly in the ointment is that they also expect after-sales service with the same ease of access.

When the online presence is just starting off, it may be possible to offer only limited frequently asked questions, a single e-mail address and a phone number that is answered only during working hours. As the business grows, these soon appear inadequate and have to be upgraded with professional tools that allow e-Service.

Examples of e-Service tools

In increasing degrees of complexity, these are as follows:

Self-service

In addition to upgrading the FAQ files, it is possible to offer an on-site search engine that can be used by customers with queries on anything ranging from the technical specifications of the product to the background of the CEO. Customers can also be invited to submit FAQs, which will be answered and listed on the site.

Increasingly sophisticated alternatives, in the form of virtual helpers, are now appearing on online presences, allowing questions to be answered in a more personalised manner, using natural language, while offering alternatives if the initial response was not relevant or suitable.

E-mail response management

This suite of tools goes well beyond the common 'help@organisation.com' type of e-mail which is a regular feature on most start-up sites. E-mail response management systems allow:

- automated responses to e-mail or web forms with predetermined answers;
- messages to be filtered by priority, e.g. a complaint will rate higher than a thank you;
- routing of difficult queries, e.g. those with more than one question, to specified individuals;

- maintenance of an audit trail of communications from immediate query to final resolution;
- analysis of e-mail traffic by any criteria, e.g. volume, agent, subject, etc.

Live help

This could take several forms, for example a link which, when clicked by the customer, sets up a real-time chat session. The human being at the other end can answer the customer's questions, forward supporting information and even slip in a subtle sales message. The advantage is that a customer with a single dial-up line does not have to disconnect from the Internet.

Alternatively, a 'Call Me' button will allow a customer to forward their phone number details and the preferred time for the live operator to call.

All the above solutions can be found in an integrated e-Service suite, and purchased on a modular basis as and when justified by the volume of service requests.

Follow up, follow up, follow up

If, despite the best technical architecture and streamlined processes, things do go wrong, it is essential to follow up the customer complaint through to resolution as soon as possible.

Given the absence of a physical presence, failure to service a complaint effectively raises a disproportionate level of doubt about an online organisation's competence. The problem is compounded by two perceptions: first, that instantaneous communications such as e-mail will generate an instant response, which is not often practical; second, that the issue being discussed is, at least in the customer's mind, important and may involve the return of one of his prized possessions – his money.

Auto-acknowledgements of inbound e-mails can provide a minimum level of comfort in confirming that the e-mail carrying the complaint has actually been received by the organisation, but that will not be enough. Only a solution will suffice.

Smother anger with a blanket of affection

The manner in which complaints are managed can either build or kill a business. The flames of anger that accompany complaints are best smothered in a blanket of affection.

In addition to resolving the problem as quickly as possible, it is always a good idea to offer the customer an item of value 'absolutely free' in recognition of the inconvenience caused. This would apply irrespective of whether or not the organisation was actually at fault in the matter. This modest gesture should create an advocate of the business, keen to share his victory and the organisation's kindness with the world at large.

Little gestures do mean a lot – as long as they're the right ones

The concept of 'free' token gestures can be deployed even outside the environment of customers with complaints. The objective is to surprise and delight by exceeding the expected level of service.

Rather than offering discounts, which then become the norm and affect the organisation's profitability, take one-off actions that cost little but mean a lot. For example, upgrade the normal delivery from mail to courier if the customer had phoned in and expressed a sense of urgency. Make no charge for the upgrade and make sure the customer sees the generosity.

The modest cost of the upgrade should be repaid several times over, not only by the customer being converted from a one-time user to a repeat purchaser, but also by new visitors, drawn by his impressive tale of customer service.

If it is possible to trace a new business referral to a specific customer, it is very important to thank the referrer. Again, this should not be in the form of cash, as it could end up commercialising future expectations of the arrangement, but another token of appreciation. This might take the form of a personalised thank-you note from a senior executive within the organisation.

Allow integrated, multi-channel conversations

Customers may see the offline and online presences of an organisation as one – especially if they share the same brand. They would expect to start, continue and conclude a conversation through any combination of channels at their disposal.

The absence of a fully integrated, multi-channel conversation facility will become apparent very quickly in the life of a growing e-Brand, and create negative impressions. Consider just two scenarios, for example:

- Customers would view the corporation as incompetent and inefficient if they could not obtain an online update on the status of an order placed via the retail outlet.

- They are likely to be annoyed and angry if requested to complete and return a printed form when they had provided the information earlier online.

Solutions vary. At a minimum, offline customers can be given access to online channels, and vice versa – while advising them that the two systems operate independently.

Alternatively, technologies such as data warehouses can be employed to consolidate data and make it accessible via any channel. Intelligent systems integration would probably represent the ideal, subject to the compatibility and extensibility of the technology used in both worlds.

Avoid technological arrogance

While just about every piece of real-world marketing collateral points a visitor to the online world, there is no reciprocal behaviour from the online presence. This is just one example of technological arrogance endemic in the online world and has a detrimental effect on business.

Often, the only alternative for payment is an online order form requiring credit card details. Yet the simple addition of mail, phone or fax orders, with payment by cheque, could materially increase revenues. Costs could be minimised by outsourcing this activity to an appropriate bureau.

Technological arrogance manifests itself in other ways as well. The use of cutting-edge technology by IT personnel when building the online presence, without any consideration for end users, is well documented in case studies worldwide. The price paid by the organisation for offers rendered invisible by technology on customers' browsers or impossibly long download times is not just the loss in revenue. It is also the damage to the e-Brand on bulletin boards and in forums around the world.

However, if a specific technology is pivotal to the use of the site, say for security reasons, then customer service personnel should be trained in guiding customers through the downloading and installation process. Simply referring customers to the appropriate site, or even sending a CD without offering 'live' installation support, may not suffice.

Make it easy to part with money

Once the customer has decided to make the purchase, facilitate the closing of the deal by placing all necessary pricing and delivery information in an easy-to-find location and explain all terms and conditions in language that is easy to digest. The result – increased sales and satisfied customers.

Welcome back, stranger

One key pitfall to avoid is the use of jargon and acronyms, especially if they refer to internal organisational terminology. Not only does it signify to the user that they are effectively 'outsiders', but it also prevents them from completing the tasks that will either turn visitors into customers, or one-time customers into long-term profit centres.

Don't assume – ask!

Business is best conducted in a feedback loop, wherein the organisation's actions result in customer feedback, which is then used to influence the next set of actions.

But this feedback often needs to be invited, as the only uninvited feedback is complaints which are not representative of the online experience of the majority of customers.

It is good practice to ask customers what they want from your online presence. Implicit in the e-Brand experience is that the site will always be available, fully functional and easily navigable, and will offer a 'customised' solution. But how, precisely, would customers like to see this executed?

One way to get closer to the customer ideal is to ask a representative group of the organisation's best customers to evaluate new releases before they go live and invite suggestions for improvement.

Implementing and rewarding the best suggestions by public recognition on the site (with the customer's permission, of course!) also goes to demonstrate 'listening' and builds trust by positioning the online presence as a business partner who is prepared to accept constructive criticism. This will also help the e-Brand evolve from the default 'here's what we have to sell' to a more solution-based 'what do you need and how can we help?'.

Although business books on the subject of customer satisfaction are helpful, there is no substitute for leaving the office and observing the target audience interacting with the online presence in the comfort of their own environment.

Add a human touch – and a dose of reality

Online presences are often rendered impersonal, despite the best design and navigation strategies. They can, however, be given a human touch in the form of photographs and 'personal' messages from employees to customers.

There are some downsides – executive search firms and recruitment consultancies find such displays to be happy hunting grounds for new candidates, and some employees may be of the view that their photographs on the Internet pose an unacceptable personal security risk.

Another suggestion might be to include a webcam of the view, say, within the reception area or immediately outside the office, as a way of indicating a physical presence in an increasingly virtual world.

PARTNERING

The Internet is the perfect example of an interconnected world. Such interconnection should extend to the online business model used by an organisation, because it is neither wise nor necessary to produce every single product or service that comprises the online offering.

It is essential, however, that the integration of a partner's complementary products and services be undertaken in a manner that allows access seamlessly to the end user. This should be done preferably without leaving, or at least appearing to leave, the initial site.

White label

A novel form of partnering involves the use of white label suppliers, wherein the bulk of the functionality is provided by a third party, and the organisation simply creates its own branded front end. Customers may not be aware that they are actually interfacing with a third party's system and personnel.

From the perspective of the organisation, such an arrangement allows for a quicker time to market with reduced capital outlay. Payment to the white label supplier is usually a combination of a monthly fee and a graduated scale of charges depending upon the number of transactions conducted through the system.

However, the e-Branding implications can be considerable. These include the following:

- *Potential confusion* – if the white label supplier insists on presenting their name and logo on the organisation's site (similar to the 'Intel Inside' strategy), customers might be unclear as to their relationship with this third party.

- *Homogenisation* – if the white label supplier offers a similar service to the organisation's competitors, the only difference between the offerings would be the home page and the frame within which the white label supplier's system operates.

- *Reduced functionality* – if the white label supplier also operates a business in the same market space as the organisation, they may choose to offer only a subset of the total functionality of the system, so as not to create competition for their own customer base.

- *Limited data* – the volume, quality and timeliness of the data on the organisation's customers held by the white label supplier may affect the organisation's e-Brand building activities.

- *Differing objectives* – the organisation's e-Branding strategy might call for expansion into new product categories or geographies, which may not be consistent with those of the white label supplier. Alternatively, even if the objectives were identical, the white label supplier may not have the resources to deliver them to the organisation's preferred timescale.

- *Service standards* – the most tightly drawn service level agreements cannot disguise the fact that the organisation's e-Brand is effectively at the mercy of the white label supplier's ability to deliver a timely, accurate and quality service.

Today's market alliance could be tomorrow's headache

Another form of partnering could take the form of market alliances. In this scenario, two or more organisations collaborate, often with brand reinforcing partners. Such alliances are announced in a blaze of publicity and the market capitalisations of both entities usually benefit as a result – for a short time, at least.

e-Branding issues arise because such alliances are relatively easy to form and in the white heat of competition, compromises might be made to arrive at a deal with the dot com flavour of the month. It is only when problems arise that the full implications of the haste begin to be realised. For example, the dot com might suffer a fall in fortunes, or insufficient resources might have been allocated to the alliance, leading to a noticeable failure to deliver.

Not surprisingly, customers who fail to obtain redress from the alliance focus their anger on the individual partners, leading to damage within their respective brands.

Even when the alliance does well, it may sometimes struggle to create its own e-Brand identity, as it is difficult to emerge from the shadows of partners who are recognised brand leaders in their own market space.

Co-branding is great, until found guilty by association

Co-branding is a variation on the market alliance theme, except that both parties lend their current names to the new co-branded entity. Unfortunately, the moment one of the co-branded entities receives some bad press, it rubs off on the other, under the principle of 'guilty by association'.

Even if both parties do well individually, shifting market conditions might require one of them to change direction to ensure their survival, leaving the other, and the co-branded venture, in an untenable position.

Breaking up co-branded ventures is also more difficult, even when details such as ownership of customer databases and sharing of future revenue streams have been negotiated in advance.

Catch them young

Partnering does not have to be restricted to other businesses which offer complementary goods or services. It can even extend to customers – or at least those who are likely to become customers in the fullness of time.

If relevant, it would be a good idea to create a section within the online presence that allows younger visitors to benefit from the site – for example, university research funding or career guidance material. By keeping these visitors in touch with the e-Brand from an early age, the online presence is effectively building relationships with future customers – or employees.

It is worth remembering that this audience will have grown up with the Internet and are far likelier to take offence at content they deem patronising or presentation they consider simplistic. Care must also be taken when communicating with minors, so as not to breach any regulatory or industry guidelines.

Protecting an e-Brand

Assuming an organisation has established and grown its e-Brand, it will repay dividends for shareholders – and unscrupulous others.

The brand name or trade and service marks could be used, for example, to embellish the perceived financial standing of fraudsters, before they fleece their victims. And the organisation is left to deal with the backlash. Constant vigilance will minimise this possibility, and the investment in prevention will be cheaper, on balance, than the remedy.

Why is this necessary? As mentioned earlier, the Internet is a great leveller, and aside from the well-known brand names, the size of the corporation behind the presence is not distinguishable.

Finally, these external circumstances are fuelled by a substantial number of self-inflicted injuries, caused by rapidly changing economic and technological landscapes.

This chapter of the Executive Briefing will help you protect one of the most valuable assets possessed by an organisation – its e-Brand!

SOFTWARE SNARLS

Are you open for business?

The online world operates 24 hours a day, 7 days a week, 365 days a year and it expects an organisation's online presence to do the same. So, how does it determine whether the organisation is open for business? Some of the components that will determine the answer include:

- Access – is the ISP fully operational and can the site be accessed?
- Internal mobility – are all the intra-site links operational?
- Navigation – is the site more intuitive and easy to navigate than before?
- Freshness – is there fresh content? Can visitors find it?

The only people more interested in the site than the owners are the competition, who visit it daily. If they spot a weakness, and notice it being repeated, they will have been handed a moral – and possibly financial – victory without a battle.

Truth, the whole truth, and nothing but the truth

Historically, organisations could assume their customer relationship as trusted service providers offered them a controlled, and one-way, communication channel for their sales and PR messages. No longer. It is now virtually impossible to hide problems with an online presence.

An alternative solution for non-transactional sites might be to openly acknowledge the problems being experienced temporarily on the site. Not only will this display of honesty enhance trust, but it has the cost benefit of cutting down the huge volume of inbound e-mail from hundreds of site users, intent on alerting the organisation to a known problem. An approximate time by which the issue should be resolved – and an apology – might also help.

Transactional sites, especially those involved in issues of personal finance and health, might find this approach inappropriate, as it may raise data security and privacy concerns that are disproportionate to the problem.

Can you replicate customers' complaints?

Customers will complain about your online presence. A one-off complaint might be specific to that customer, but multiple complaints around the same issue might be indicative of a deeper problem, often technological.

There is an urgency involved that transcends customer service issues. The degree of automation inherent in online presences means that technical issues have the unfortunate habit of replicating at speed and creating further data corruption problems in downstream applications and processes.

This, in turn, makes the problem visible, and quickly, to a far larger audience than would have been possible in the real world. The sooner the customers' complaints can be replicated – and resolved – the lesser the possibility of IT personnel having the additional burden of explaining their actions to senior management.

Beware the 'pick-n-mix' school of website building

Business users often point to their favourite websites to explain their aspirations for their own organisation's site – and in lieu of detailed functional specifications that are unique to the organisation.

This 'pick-n-mix' school of website building has two fundamental negatives. First, the end result always displeases everyone – because the organisation ends up with a horse that looks like a zebra and operates like a donkey. Worse still, the essence of the e-Brand will be lost, and the online presence will appear to be nothing more than a mosaic of its competitors.

Fresh starts are OK – just don't forget existing customers

Freshening up an online presence is a laudable objective and, depending upon the industry, should be undertaken at least every couple of years.

In the interim, there will invariably be incremental enhancements. Treating these like a fresh start will simply delay implementation and demonstrates a disregard for a valuable asset – existing customers. While the existing layout and navigation may be less than perfect, at least it is familiar to users, particularly newer Internet arrivals, who fear change more than others. Incremental changes should be just that – incremental.

Prior to the implementation of the fresh start, existing users should be notified, and some even offered the opportunity to test-drive the new presence to determine how it differs from the old, and whether the transition to the newer model is a smooth one.

Of course, even the smallest enhancement has implications for the underlying code used to build the online presence. Rigorous release procedures should be in place to ensure version control, and to enable the system to revert to the last fully operational version in an emergency, if required.

Eliminating existing pages should be a cause for concern. Some users may have bookmarked them, and regular customers may choose to enter the site other than at the home page. In either case, missing or broken links destroy some of the advantages that would otherwise have been gained by the new presence.

Test, test, test

If the three golden rules for investing in property are location, location and location, then the three golden rules for avoiding self-inflicted injuries online must be test, test and test again – before putting a new release 'live'.

Invariably, competitive pressures, poor business-led specifications and executive decision-making delays contribute to a mad dash to issue the next release. Unless the organisation will be in breach of a regulatory requirement or one of its self-appointed policies, releases should not be launched without testing.

Security is cheap at double the price

The cost of security breaches invariably outweighs the cost of implementing security procedures at the outset. Some of the cost may not initially be in physical pounds and pence but in adverse publicity – which is often worse for transactional sites than informational sites.

Even obsolescence is valuable

Often, pages within the online presence are hyperlinked from other pages on the Internet and bookmarked by users. Changing or deleting the pages to which these hyperlinks and bookmarks connect could destroy a valuable source of future traffic.

If, however, a change absolutely has to be made, the new version of the page should be released in both the old and new locations – or the old re-directed to the new.

By keeping obsolete web pages alive, existing users are spared the frustration of updating their links and the organisation is assured of future traffic.

MARKETING MAYHEM

Deliver the promise, not just the product or service

All too often, millions of pounds are spent on advertising and marketing in the name of 'brand building'. It is important to recognise that all that is being achieved is temporary brand awareness, not brand loyalty. The latter only arises after repeated usage of the online service, resulting in pleasant customer experiences on each occasion. This also raises the level of trust, leading customers to forgive the occasional hiccup in performance.

Put customers in the driving seat

The key factors that should determine the speed and direction of an organisation's journey online are the availability – to users, not employees – of the following:

- ability to receive and understand promotional material sent online;
- ability to order online;
- ability to pay online;
- ability to seek assistance and customer service online.

Respect Internet culture

Commonly referred to as 'netiquette', respecting certain behavioural norms on the Internet is more than just good manners. It indicates an understanding of the medium, which in turn allows users to place greater trust in the e-Brand.

This ranges from subtle issues such as not using CAPITAL LETTERS in e-mail communication (which represents shouting) to sending large graphic files that could result in considerable dial-up charges when downloaded.

Even the freedom offered by the Internet should be used wisely – especially freedom of speech. In the real world, there are checks and balances – for example, does the freedom of speech extend to falsely shouting 'Fire' in a crowded auditorium knowing it could result in injury or death for stampeding innocents?

Who are you – and why should I trust you?

The creators of an online presence could be forgiven for wondering why their well-designed, easily navigable and regularly visited site fails to generate sales. The answer might lie in the fact that nowhere on the site is there a mention of a single human being. No name, no photograph, no direct line number – just an impersonal e-mail address.

Organisations which recognise this shortcoming and apply a human face to the Web might just be in for a surprise. Pages showing the names, photographs and short messages from senior executives are often the ones visited prior to the decision to purchase. The fact that the pages exist may, for some, be enough of a comfort factor.

There are some issues with this approach – some personnel may feel the exposure represents a personal security risk, and executive search firms will be able to lure talent faster as they already have some background information. On balance, however, the decision to humanise the online presence will pay dividends over time.

Turn dead-ends into referrals

Sometimes an organisation's site will be accessed by people who have absolutely no interest in the products or services being offered. If they arrived there because of misleading claims in a link elsewhere, they are unlikely to be pleased. However, if the arrival was by chance, they may see something of value for a friend. If the online presence has a mechanism for allowing them to refer the site to the friend before they exit, an initial dead-end can be turned into a potentially valuable referral.

Trapped in a time warp

Technology is available for profiling users – using a combination of information they volunteered and that gathered by an organisation during their use of its online presence.

Unfortunately, too many organisations consider this initial collection of data the Holy Grail of online marketing and continue marketing using this profile well past its sell-by date. A student who registered with the site three years ago is probably now an income-earning employee. Yet the organisation insists on making student-related offers, trapping the person in a profile from which it is impossible to escape.

Old experience + New technology = Success

There is a strong case for hiring old-school direct marketers to form part of the online marketing team. Part of the reason is that the similarities between offline direct marketing and online e-Marketing are considerable – short, sharp copy, immediacy of action, measurable results, etc.

But perhaps the most important reason is to prevent the kinds of mistakes that result in e-Brand damage. E-mail campaigns sent to the wrong people, reply addresses that don't work, new offers that only customers (but not employees) know about – all these, and more, could have been prevented by an experienced direct marketer who would have been aware of their real-world equivalents.

What's more, once direct marketers become comfortable with the new technology, they are likely to suggest innovative, yet responsive campaigns, and make the organisation's product or service look more attractive than any technologist could do.

One lesson they need to learn very rapidly, however, is that repetition does not work. In real-world media, marketing communications are repeated constantly to build brand awareness. In the online world, this suggests limited imagination and stale content.

Traps are for rats, not customers

Technology will forever create new toys and marketers are always ready to play. One such device is the interstitial – literally 'in between'.

In theory, this means an advertisement that appears in a separate browser while the page requested by the user is in the process of being downloaded. If appealing, the user can take a detour and respond to the advertisement prior to returning to the business at hand.

In practice, interstitials carry large graphics, sound files and Java applets, making them a downloading nightmare and delaying access to the destination page even further. Users who minimise the interstitial suddenly realise they have lost their original browser – and eventually work out that they have to close the interstitial first, or re-click on the original browser. All of which leaves the user feeling like a trapped rat – confused and unhappy.

One positive use of interstitials, however, is to inform users upon arrival at the site of a major development such as a website redesign or an emergency problem. Keeping the graphics to a minimum and explaining how the user can exit the interstitial will allow this device to be used as intended.

Committing e-Brand suicide

Despite all the knowledge increasingly available on the dos and don'ts of online marketing, organisations insist on committing e-Brand suicide in a variety of ways:

■ *Mocking today's Internet illiterate customers.* The real-world customer being mocked and pilloried in today's advertising campaign will avoid the organisation's site like the plague when online in the future. An organisation should also be careful about predicting the demise of its real-world competitors, as it may have to merge with them in the not too distant future.

■ *Under construction.* It is widely recognised that every online presence is under constant maintenance and updating on a daily basis. There is no need or justification for using icons such as 'Under Construction' or 'Updated Soon'. The closest real-world equivalent would be sending customers a letter advising them that the catalogue they are due to receive is still being produced.

■ *Advertising inadequacies.* These fall into three categories:

- *Offers inconsistent with brand* – attempting to take advantage of a short-term promotional opportunity by co-branding with an inappropriate partner. The short-term gain, if any, will be more than offset by long-term e-Brand damage.

- *Unsubstantiated claims* – unlike the real world, these will find their way to the local regulatory, consumer or TV-based watchdog within a matter of minutes. The wasted investment in any marketing literature is insignificant compared with the time cost of dampening down the flames of adverse publicity.

- *Being over-clever* – this is when a 'clever' idea, conceived over a late night creative session, proves to be less than intelligent in the cold light of consumer disgust.

It's no longer a game

Using online games as an involvement device and a means of building e-Brands is fraught with danger – even for fun-loving, lifestyle brands.

First, the fact that an online presence is global invariably means that one set of rules is unlikely to be legally acceptable in all the countries from which users are expected to participate.

Then there are religious objections, which rule out games of chance in certain parts of the world. When coupled with social norms which disallow promotions or prizes presented by scantily clad persons, the room for manoeuvre is considerably limited.

Finally, any reward involving cash – or a cash equivalent – ceases to make it a game altogether. Worse still, it turns the involvement device into a stick with which sore losers beat the organisation's e-Brand well after the 'game' has ended.

Conflict resolution rules

With promotional activities occurring both online and offline, it is increasingly likely that there will be a conflict between the sales offers, terms of business and speed of delivery – which could disadvantage some customers.

The difference might be intentional, e.g. a price difference, with a saving for ordering on the Internet. Alternatively, it could be as a result of a mistake, e.g. a printed order form specifies a closing date for a special offer, yet it is still possible to access that offer via the online presence of the same organisation after the deadline.

In either case, a clear explanation and a customer-friendly solution would go some considerable way towards limiting the e-Brand damage. Given the inevitability of the situation, having the conflict resolution rules in place from the outset would save having to scramble around for a company policy on the issue during each occurrence, and minimise the delay in responding to customers.

In fact, if managed correctly, it could even turn the situation into a selling opportunity. For example, the customer who placed the order offline could still be offered the saving if they agreed to open an online account.

Do you know your customer well enough?

Organisations expect their customers to know everything about their brand. Yet different departments within an organisation are likely to have widely differing perceptions about, and behaviours towards, their best customers.

Part of the solution lies in interdepartmental coordination and seamless data transfers between channels. Among other things, this saves customers having to provide the same data more than once.

While this may be grudgingly tolerated in the offline world, any impression of 'missing' data is likely to damage trust-based relationships beyond repair in the online world.

Big Brother is watching

The flip side of the 'missing' data coin are the e-Brand abuses committed in the name of 'personalisation'. Demonstrating to customers that the organisation is aware of their every move or need, simply because of the volume of data held on them, is another recipe for disaster.

For example, a discreet prompt to consider school fees planning is likely to generate a far more favourable reaction than listing the names and dates of birth of a customer's children simply because this information is available to the organisation.

The truth behind 'stickiness'

But there is an even greater truth – customers are made 'sticky' not because of the volume of data an organisation holds *on* them, but *for* them.

Data held *on* customers means they can be greeted with a personalised message when they next visit the online presence. That, in itself, will not be enough to prevent them leaving for a competitor's special offer.

The stickiness lies in customers' realisation that they will have to transfer, and re-key, all the data about their requirements currently held *for* them by the organisation's online presence. That's when apathy and time pressures come to the rescue of the organisation's e-Brand.

Make unbeatable, but credible, offers

Converting prospects into customers so they can interact with the e-Brand and become loyal and profitable advocates requires the first step to be made – converting prospects into sales. This can be achieved by making credible offers – and guaranteeing them. A 100 per cent refund would be such an example.

But it is possible to make the offer even more attractive by including a gift or bonus item with the original offer. Should the customer express dissatisfaction, not only will they receive a 100 per cent refund but they are free to keep the bonus item.

Prospects have to take the view that the offer entails no risk for them and should take that all-important first step towards conversion into customers.

Before you go...

Dissatisfied customers are a loss to the organisation at several levels. Not only do they represent a revenue stream lost, but they could also share their dissatisfaction with other potential customers.

An organisation should attempt to extract one last item of value from departing customers – the reason for their dissatisfaction. This silent killer, once identified, can be neutralised and other losses contained.

If handled effectively, customers could be impressed with the attention provided and choose not to leave after all – a double victory.

ORGANISATIONAL OBSTACLES

Revolutions have a way of becoming evolutions when size and bureaucracy enter the operational world of a nimble dot com – as they must at some stage of the development of the business.

But there are other organisational obstacles that stand in the way of developing a strong e-Brand – and which require strong leadership and teaming skills if they are to be overcome:

- While the trend towards convergence between online and offline companies makes synergistic sense, it carries an implicit assumption – that the corporate cultures of the two organisations will be able to work together as a cohesive whole. Sensitivities will be heightened if the new entity discards one or both of the existing brands in favour of a new one.

- Cultural differences may exist even within the organisation, especially between the front-line marketing personnel and their real-world back-end counterparts who process the results of their efforts. The former thrive on entrepreneurial flair and the latter on attention to detail. The former invariably accuse the latter of resistance to change, and the latter accuse the former of acting without thinking through the consequences. Add to this heady mix the contempt held by IT for anyone who cannot tell the difference between XML and HTML and the result is an uneasy truce at the best of times.

- The role of IT is further diffused as they are increasingly – and in some cases, unnecessarily – being forced to become customer facing. With customers expecting instant responses to technology-related questions, the customer service department often takes the soft option – redirecting the e-mail or phone call to IT. Unfortunately, IT personnel have not been trained in customer service skills, resulting in a variable range of responses all the way up to 'you're too stupid to own a computer!'. A better solution would be to improve the base technology knowledge of customer service personnel, and refer genuinely difficult questions to a pre-selected contact within IT.

- Even in the online world it is possible to destroy a business without going on strike – simply continue to offer the churlish service customers are accustomed to in the offline world. For example, insisting upon evidence of despatch of returned goods may make sense for a warehouse clerk, but it also implies the customer is dishonest. Subject only to unacceptable commercial risk, it is worth offering the customer the benefit of the doubt.

- Outsourcing is a way of life for online-only businesses, as existing personnel and resources make running the operation from front to back a near impossibility. The difficulty here is convincing the outsourced operation to operate at the same level of customer service as that promised by the organisation's e-Brand to its customers.

While the above issues may appear daunting, it is possible to ease the pain through regular, clear and honest communication between departments and between senior and junior employees. The litmus test for the marketing department is reasonably easy: are all relevant employees aware – and have they had the opportunity to comment on – the latest offer before it is made public?

FOUL PLAY

Every brand has an Achilles heel

The key question is – can it be overcome, and if so, how? Threats to the e-Brand can originate from internal or external sources. Internally, they usually revolve around personnel – for example, loss of key staff.

External factors could range from a stock market crash that affects the next round of funding through to changing regulatory or political regimes.

Independence of infomediaries

Customers' reliance on information intermediaries to provide assistance or background information prior to making purchasing decisions is fine – except that some infomediaries may not be entirely independent or may have hidden agendas.

If any of them are unreasonably hostile to the organisation, their motives should be investigated further.

If it sounds too good to be true...

If it sounds too good to be true, it probably is. This old adage, from the offline world, is just as appropriate in the online world.

Except that consumers are so accustomed to receiving incredible offers from online start-ups their normal scepticism is often suspended. In the rush to build market share, start-ups have clearly bribed visitors to become customers. This may have taken the form of gifts or subsidising costs which would otherwise have had to be borne by the customer.

This has, unfortunately, also left the door wide open for fraudsters, who make equally incredible offers, except they have no intention of delivering a product or service for the funds provided. It is no use crying caveat emptor – buyer beware – because as long as there are people out there willing to pay for burial plots on Mars, there will be fraudsters willing to supply them.

However, as fraud-related pain increases for consumers in general, over-generous offers will be tarred with the same brush – a point that should be borne in mind when crafting the next 'incredible' offer.

Abandon hope if you abandoned your URL

Some online presences have chosen a new name, identity and URL. This is the real-world equivalent of changing a business's physical address, phone and fax number. Except that the implications could be considerable.

While most online presences will redirect viewers to their new address, others abandon the old address to save a few pounds on the domain registration charges. Unfortunately, the abandoned domain can then be snapped up by unsavoury alternatives such as pornography suppliers or, worse still, a direct competitor.

Turn fraud concerns to your advantage

It is possible to turn fraud-related concerns to the advantage of the organisation. First, with every e-mail campaign enclose a hyperlink that returns the visitor to a jump page (also known as a splash page) on the site.

This special page is set up to let visitors know they are indeed dealing with the organisation that despatched the e-mail, and could remind them of the salient features of the offer. Thereafter, it can allow them to register or log into the core of the site.

Where possible, a customer services phone number should be clearly visible, allowing the truly cautious – or nervous – visitor to become increasingly comfortable with dealing on the site.

Misuse of Internet reference systems

This covers a whole series of sins, some of which could inadvertently involve your e-Brand, and ranges among the following:

- Operating domains based on potential mis-spellings of popular domain names.
- Copying meta-tags from sites that rank highly in search engines.
- Unauthorised framing of other sites' material within an organisation's site to borrow credibility, imply a commercial relationship or use copyright material without payment.
- IP cloaking or stealth scripting – presenting a search engine with a page specially customised to allow the site to be rated highly, yet re-routing customers to another page within the site, or another site altogether when they click the link from the search engine results page. Legitimate websites use this to prevent their meta-tags being stolen and misused by others, although search engines disapprove as it affects the integrity of the search function.
- Page-jacking (also known as page-napping) – occurs when a substantial part of a site is copied and stored on a rogue web server. The server is registered with

an address similar to the one copied and submitted to search engines. Users linking from search engine results believe they are in the original site, only to discover that the links from the page-jacked site connect to places of questionable morality or legality.

■ Spoofing – occurs when a malicious party reconfigures a DNS server (a computer that acts as the address book for networks) to pass all traffic to or from that site via its computers. Sensitive data such as passwords, credit card details, etc. are then extracted from the traffic. This technique is sometimes combined with page-jacking, where the user voluntarily enters sensitive data, having been led to believe that the site is the original one requested.

Never allow a free ride

An organisation that has paid to build an e-Brand may find it being hijacked for purposes other than simply counterfeiting or adulteration. These include the illegal use of brand names, trade and service marks in meta-tags to attract higher search engine rankings. Alternatively, brand names are simply attached to sites to imply a trading relationship or an unjustified impression of financial stability or used in chat rooms and newsgroups for the same purpose.

The key issue is that after a customer has been parted from his money, the only memorable elements are the legitimate brands used for illegal purposes by third parties.

Services that track such e-Brand abuses are now available and enforcement usually commences with threatening the site's owners with legal action. If this fails, the action can be extended to include the offending site's Internet service provider – as an accessory to the crime – which often has the desired effect of having the offending site terminated.

Although it is also possible to prevent unauthorised copying of websites and include digital watermarks in audio and graphic files, the requirements for users to download special plug-ins are quite onerous.

Also, search engine robots cannot enter such secure sites, meaning that they will never be ranked and effectively leave the site owner with a difficult choice – potential theft of the e-Brand or security at the expense of obscurity.

Guerrilla marketing

This increasingly abused term should refer to the use of streetwise tactics to achieve, on a budget, the same level of results and exposure normally associated with huge marketing spends.

Over time, it has increasingly become associated with techniques that skirt the boundaries of legality and raise ethical questions. Some examples of guerrilla marketing to date include the following:

- Identifying visitors from a competitor using their IP address and routing them directly to the 'jobs available' section of the site, with a view to poaching the competitor's staff.

- Entering a chat room under a false identity, asking a question, leaving the chat room, re-entering it under a second false identity, and answering the question with either a criticism of a competitor or offering a link to the organisation's site.

- Leading an online forum, during which questions are requested from the online audience. Irrespective of the questions actually asked, only those pre-scripted, with answers showing the organisation in a favourable light, are actually transmitted.

- Choosing a competitor's name as the keyword on a popular search engine, ensuring that every time it is included in the search query, the resulting advertising banner served is that of the organisation.

- Offering only competitors' customers a generous incentive to switch business to the organisation – on the basis that the cost of the incentive will still be cheaper than the huge acquisition cost in identifying and assessing the suitability of the customer, which has already been borne by the competitor.

POLICY PROTECTION

Simply having policies is not enough

Given the well publicised concerns about security, data protection and privacy online, it is important to have policies covering these areas. It is even more important to be seen to be complying with them. For example, explaining to customers that the padlock icon they see when entering their password proves their data is being transmitted in a secure manner does wonders for building trust.

What's more, these policies should be given pride of place, wherever appropriate. Placing a copyright statement on the site explicitly stating copyright of the contents implies the site contains items of value that will be vigorously defended by the owner.

Other trust-building initiatives include offering policy explanations in both technical and non-technical formats, allowing, say, non-technically literate users to understand how the secure sockets layer (SSL) protocol works to protect their data.

Privacy policies are almost mandatory

In countries where data protection legislation does not exist (yet!), privacy policies play a crucial role in the credibility of the e-Brand.

Absence of a privacy policy – a statement on the collection, storage and use of personal data – increasingly weighs upon the decision as to whether or not a site should be trusted.

And the pressure is increasing. New services rate the privacy policies at various online presences. A poor ranking, especially from an independent agency, will take the e-Brand some time to recover.

Accidental violations

Despite the best will in the world, it is quite possible that regulations or stated policies can be accidentally violated. For example, an organisation may not be in a position to offer financial services outside its home jurisdiction but has forgotten to include a disclaimer to this effect.

As long as these accidental violations are put right immediately upon identification and the affected customers sent an intelligently crafted explanatory note, the damage should be confinable.

The silver lining

There may be a small silver lining to the privacy cloud. Customers are now able to use web services that anonymise their identity online, allowing them not to be tracked as they go from site to site.

While this may result in the loss of tracking intelligence for the organisation, early findings are that the customers' comfort in the anonymity of online purchases is increasing access to their wallets at a faster pace than most sales pitches could achieve.

RATING RAT-RACE

Ratings influence revenues

As if e-Brands didn't have enough to worry about – changing regulatory and economic landscapes and aggressive competitors – a new form of threat has emerged. Ratings – whether formalised or informal – increasingly have the power to direct large sums of revenue from one organisation to another.

The worrying part is that the person behind the ratings could be ill-informed, opinionated and simply wrong – yet an Internet connection is all that is needed to wield this enormous power.

Before moving to the various forms of external ratings, it is worth considering if – and how – it is possible to set up some internal barometers.

Self-ratings are only worth it if you're honest!

The underlying principle is one of measurement. As with direct marketing in the real world, if an organisation does not monitor and measure results, success will be impossible to determine.

Measurement should cover quantitative measures such as sales and market share, as well as qualitative measures such as perceived changes in the brand essence as discussed in structured focus groups.

These should be complemented with a map of the competitive landscape, whereby the product and service features associated with the organisation's brand are compared with those of competitors across various facets. These include geographic availability, product range, value for money, etc.

Mystery shopping should be taken to the level where honest comparisons can be made between competitors' claimed offerings and the performance – in real life – of the features and functionality.

Such close monitoring should also allow identification of micro-competitors – who normally slip under the radar – and the areas in which they are chipping away at the organisation's e-Brand piece by piece. The problem with micro-competitors is not their size. It is the fact that they compete on sub-sets of functionality, which may be overwhelmingly important to some customers, resulting in their defection.

Finally, a brand audit on each brand within a family should help address how well they are functioning within the overall context of the organisation's objectives, their usage, performance and variations from patterns of expected behaviour. Where the latter is due to one-off circumstances, the matter can be allowed to rest. If not, an investigation into the causes for the variation should be examined very carefully.

In all cases, total honesty is required from the organisation in evaluating its own progress. If this is not possible for internal political reasons, an external agency should be engaged for the task.

Formal rating agencies

External ratings take several forms. Formal ratings agencies exist in the real world and have branched into online ratings as well. Their detailed findings are only available on a 'paid-for' basis, and are relied upon by decision-makers in corporations ranging from venture capital funds to joint venture partners.

It is wise to understand the precise basis – and methodology – used by such agencies, and to present subsequent years' data in a format that best suits those agencies. If the ratings are particularly favourable, they can be used as the foundation for building stature for the e-Brand, on the basis of its recognition by an independent third party.

Opinion sites

The impact of online sites devoted expressly to collating and leveraging customer opinions should not be underestimated. These often have professionals running the online presence as a full-time business, although the contributors are individuals who have purchased and used the product or service being rated.

Consumers seeking the views of other users before making purchasing decisions will visit such a site, search for the product or service by brand name and read the reviews. Readers can then rate the reviews in terms of usefulness, etc.

Consumer-to-consumer communication

Other alternatives include software packages that allow consumers to do everything from posting notes on the site visited which other users of the same software can read to forming communities around users' opinions of a particular offering. Both options are essentially giving private individuals a public voice – though admittedly only to users of the same software package. Options such as these will persist for as long as users believe they stand to obtain better value from other users' opinions rather than from the promotional material on the site of the offering.

e-Commerce aggregation and portal sites also allow customer reviews on the specific products and services they sell, allowing customers to see both the product provider's views and those of previous purchasers. While the latter may not induce a sale, a negative review has been known to dampen enthusiasm caused earlier by the promotional material.

Gripe sites

Anyone with a modicum of computer literacy can now set up a website to share their point of view with the world. This may include their dislike of a particular corporation or brand. As a result, any real or imagined grievance is likely to manifest itself as a gripe site.

In the USA, gripe sites are often registered in the format 'xyzsucks' where xyz represents the name of the corporation or brand being denigrated. As a precautionary measure, therefore, most large corporations and even famous personalities have already registered their relevant version of the 'xyzsucks' domain.

Opinion is divided about what to do next. Some advocate routing the 'xyzsucks' domain to the official site of the relevant organisation, but that would be akin to adding insult to injury. A simpler option might be to register the domain and never use it. Of course, gripe sites with less obvious names can be set up, but they will need a greater investment in time and energy to achieve the same degree of visibility as the 'xyzsucks' format. And the person setting up the site must really have to hate the e-Brand – which is increasingly the case – with formerly pacifist movements resorting to direct action to achieve their objectives.

What can be done about a gripe site? An interesting spin would be to determine whether it can be brought within the confines of the official site, i.e. offer a designated space on the official site, free of editorial interference. Not only does this position the e-Brand as a 'listening' entity, it also allows the organisation to obtain early warning of incorrectly executed strategy and to place counterbalancing views on other parts of its own site.

Newsgroups and bulletin boards

Newsgroups and bulletin boards can also be created for the purposes of posting negative comments about the e-Brand. Focusing on the more respected or higher-traffic sites would be a valuable investment of time. A decision as to whether or not to respond to negative comments, either in an official or unofficial capacity, is a judgement call that has to be made by the organisation on a case-by-case basis.

The difficulty arises because there is rarely an opportunity to question the legitimacy of claims made on such sites, and any official reaction might be interpreted as providing credibility to a comment that might otherwise have been consigned to the dustbin of history.

Links

Links to and from other websites are a form of implied endorsement and rating. Where the organisations linking to the site are unsavoury, attempts should be made to persuade them to remove the link from their site.

Levelling the playing field for minorities

First the good news. The Internet, as a medium, does not discriminate on the basis of race, colour, gender or age. Each of these special interest groups does, however, use it to promote their particular point of view.

Interestingly, when engaging in e-Commerce online, minorities tend to receive a more objective response to their interaction with the e-Brand, away from the real or perceived difficulties encountered when interfacing with the same brand in the offline world.

With the Web Accessibility Initiative from the World Wide Web Consortium (W3C) gaining momentum, people with disabilities could be enjoying a high degree of Web usability, and the same positive experiences encountered by minorities.

Action now!

Understanding why the organisation has been rated at a particular level and identifying the steps that can be taken to improve its standing is just the first step in the preservation of the e-Brand. Taking immediate action on the findings is what really counts.

FUTURE FACTORS

This chapter concludes with an examination of future-related factors that could influence the value and positioning of an e-Brand.

Disruptive displacements

The future, by definition, is uncertain. Consequently, a series of factors could result in the disruption or displacement of a carefully launched and nurtured e-Brand. Knowing about these factors could at a minimum help identify certain trends and serve as an early warning signal.

- The ingenuity of the offering's creator is bettered only by the ingenuity of the offering's destroyer. The history of the Internet to date is littered with this truism. Consider the development from a single search engine to a search engine of search engines, to natural language searches.

- Today's bright idea could be tomorrow's anti-trust investigation. The recency of some business models, and their impact on the competitive landscape, means that they could be viewed negatively further into the e-Brand's life. By taking certain precautions, such as complying with existing real-world legislation, where applicable, the chances of negative reactions can be reduced, but not eliminated.

- New disruptive technology might cause a tidal wave. While overnight obsolescence is unlikely, a genuinely effective technology might materially shorten the lifespan of the e-Brand, unless the underlying product and service offering can be modified to comply with it. For example, with automated assistants (bots) increasingly being called upon to advise on purchasing decisions strictly on the basis of objective criteria, online presences may have to be re-tuned to appeal to their rational requirements rather than the eventual purchaser's emotional requirements.

- Innovative and aggressive competition, especially from a corporation with deep pockets, might destroy an otherwise viable e-Brand before it has had the opportunity to obtain the foothold it needs for survival.

- An accidental or indefensible breach of security or privacy policies could prove to be a body blow in an otherwise stable e-Brand development cycle.

- Self-inflicted injuries always require guarding against. Prime among these is the failure to keep track of the renewal of domain name(s) and developments originating from ICANN (Internet Corporation for Assigned Names and Numbers). For example, several leading organisations have already had their domain names expire, as the notices for renewals were sent to addresses or persons no longer available. This puts them back in the pool for purchase by others. Also, with the increasing number of characters available for use in domain names and proposed new top-level domains, there is enough activity in this vital area to warrant the attention of a senior-level executive within the organisation. Where domain names show the organisation's ISP as the 'administration' or 'billing' contact, even greater care needs to be taken to ensure the domain name cannot be held hostage in future billing disputes with the ISP, and that their renewal procedures will not allow accidental cancellations.

- Revitalisation could take the form of re-branding, preferably not to cover past mistakes or an e-Brand's mid-life crisis, but as a foundation for the future. As the exercise is a substantial one in both time and money, affecting multiple real-world touch-points such as stores, stationery, etc. as well, it should not be taken lightly. It should also not be used as cover for a lack of innovation or a copycat effort of another competitor's market-moving activities.

- Tracking the future of money is essential. Without an exchange of value, there is no e-Commerce. Keeping in touch with developments in this area should leave the e-Brand well positioned to capitalise on any clear market trend. This could be in the form of an alternative to credit cards – spurred by the need for anonymity, lack of access to credit, age constraints, consumer-to-consumer payments, micropayments, and the desire to reduce the commissions payable to the card issuers. Such alternatives could take many forms – gift certificates, quasi-currencies such as 'beenz', or even mileage in frequent flyer programmes. Or the economic world could go full circle and return to barter through a series of exchanges. The victor is likely to be the solution that offers the greatest universal acceptance, liquidity, anonymity and ability to redeem value in both the online and offline worlds.

- The role of brands is changing. Whereas retail purchases are influenced by a whole series of tactile and sensory impulses, shopping on the Internet tends to be more comparison driven – given the vast amounts of data and opinions available on products within any given category. These opinions may increasingly absorb share of mind compared with the emotional pull of real-world brands – unless, of course, 3D and other technology provides new sensory interfaces online.

- Rating agencies might emerge as the new powerhouses. When brands first grew into prominence, they served as shorthand for quality and value for purchasers of a specific product. With the multiplicity of choice available nowadays, new forms of guidance are likely to be needed. These could take the form of ratings agencies, whose integrity is unquestioned by consumers. Whether these are the equivalent of today's real-world consumer associations or tomorrow's online equivalents will remain to be seen.

- Understand that hyperlinks have changed everything. No longer does information need to be sought and consumed in a linear manner. Tomorrow's version of hyperlinks could be intuitive enough to hand almost total control to the consumer over what, when, where, how and why they interact with an organisation's online presence.

Lead as model citizens in every community

Every online presence is part of several communities – whether defined by geography, industry or functionality.

Within these communities, the content and value of the online presence is important, but there is an even greater asset – reputation. The smaller the community, the greater the need to preserve the reputation – something best achieved by leading as a model citizen.

This means, among other things, paying suppliers on time, respecting self-imposed privacy and data protection policies, ensuring the security of customer data, reducing the administrative hurdles customers have to overcome when returning goods, and so on.

The model citizen approach pays dividends. In the short term, these take the form of increased sales resulting from word of mouth recommendations. In the longer term, they allow flexibility, without loss of a loyal customer base – for example, changing the business model from being the supplier of a single product to an information portal in a specialist area.

CONCLUSION

In future, the true worth of an e-Brand may well be assessed principally by how much it would cost to duplicate or exceed it. This assumes it is even possible – given the e-Brand's advantage and positioning within the marketplace, and its place in the hearts of consumers and in the memory banks of web robots.

5

Epilogue

FOLKLORE

Other ways in which an organisation's e-Brand could be damaged include relatively minor incidents that end up becoming folklore.

For example, even in December 2000, several online presences still proudly display their Y2K contingency plans, dated December 1999, accessible via a link from their home page. Or head office sites still display addresses and phone numbers of their overseas offices in formats last used a decade ago.

If the organisation can escape the insinuation that the left hand does not know what the right hand is doing, it might just be nominated for an award.

Unfortunately, some awards have a less than stellar reputation. Take, for example, a Young Businessman of the Year award, whose previous recipients have declared bankruptcy within a year of being showered with that fine accolade.

YOU WILL BE BLAMED FOR THINGS THAT ARE NOT YOUR FAULT

One of the delights of the online world is the pace of change. Previously inaccessible goods and services now fall within the range of most people with access to the Internet and a credit card.

But keeping up with the speed of change is not necessarily easy or comfortable – and as people try to adapt from the real world to the virtual, the chasm between the two is sometimes exposed.

And as we all know, the customer is always right. Table 5.1 provides some real-life examples of poor adaptation to the online world.

Table 5.1 Real-life examples of poor adaptation to the online world

Issue	Example
Technology	'I've been trying to get onto your site for hours! And no, I don't have one of those modem thingies, whatever that might be.'
Business model	'I can't add more stock to my portfolio. Are you absolutely sure you can't change the stock market price just a teeny-weeny bit for me, please?'
Functionality	'Yes, I pressed the "Order Now" button on the screen. I didn't think you'd be stupid enough to deliver 80 leather jackets to my front door. I was only practising – you know, exactly like I do in your shop when I try out some clothes before I buy them.'

TECHNOLOGY-INSPIRED CHAOS

On a slightly more complex note, here is a sequence of events explaining how technology could make life harder rather than easier, even for innocent organisations:

- An organisation sets up an auto-responder – say, an e-mail service that thanks senders for joining the e-mail subscription list and advising that their first issue will be despatched shortly.

- The auto-responder e-mail address is harvested by spider software released by people whose role in life is restricted to collecting and selling e-mail addresses in bulk.

- These e-mail addresses are then used by their new owner, a bulk purchaser of e-mail addresses. He adds to the development of e-Commerce worldwide by sending out e-mails (which includes the organisation's auto-responder, remember!) with an invitation to view pornography, get rich quick, grow taller, attract more women, enjoy a free vacation, or view even more pornography. Given his lack of technical skill, all the e-mail addresses are placed either in the To: or Cc: fields rather than the Bcc: field.

- A morally upright citizen, visibly annoyed, sends a less than polite reply to the originator of the bulk e-mail, using the 'Reply To All' button, without deleting the hundreds of e-mail addresses it already contains.

- The morally upright citizen's e-mail duly arrives at the organisation's auto-responder e-mail address which, being fully automated, reacts exactly as it was programmed to do – it sends a note thanking the citizen for joining the organisation's e-mail subscription list and advising that his first issue will be despatched shortly.

- Now, the morally upright citizen thinks the organisation has joined the list of people intent on spamming him out of existence, and sends a further irate e-mail...threatening legal action, promising to set up a gripe site against the e-Brand, etc. (By the way this storyline ignores the fact that other auto-responders and morally upright citizens are likely to be on the same bulk e-mail list, which would only add to the noise.)

- Of course, all of this can be explained once the morally upright citizen calms down, but in the meantime he has written to the organisation's top 10 trading partners identified from the organisation's site, advising them of his thoughts at being spammed. Their CEOs are now on the phone wanting to speak urgently with the organisation's CEO, as they do not wish to be associated with an indiscriminate spammer.

- And the problem goes on and on!

Glossary: Brand-related terminology

This glossary represents the generally accepted definitions of brand-related terminology.

Brand terminology	Generally accepted definition
Alignment	A process whereby the values represented by the brand are maintained in line with the actions taken, or claims made, by the brand owner.
Architecture	The structure – and the relationships – between a brand, its owners, its values and features, and the products, services or lifestyle it represents. When optimised, the potential synergies and equity-improving opportunities should be clearly visible to the brand owner.
Attitude	This represents the users' perception of what the brand thinks of them – along the lines of 'if you need to check the price, you shouldn't be buying it'. Generally speaking, attitudes of friendliness and respect will serve the brand better than arrogance except, perhaps, where an element of exclusivity is intentionally cultivated.
Attributes	Moving away from intangibles, attributes represent the real-world advantages and benefits a brand offers over its competitors.
Audit	A structured examination of the brand's usage and performance across a series of variables including geography, marketing, communications, etc. Underlying data used in the audit should be both quantitative (e.g. sales and TV exposures) and qualitative (e.g. focus group perceptions). Deviations from expected patterns, whether in usage or in results, should be investigated and remedial actions taken as necessary.
Awareness	Prompted or unprompted recall of a brand. Often used as a measure of the effectiveness of a brand's promotion campaigns.
Brand	Definitions vary according to the profession providing the answer: ■ *Legal* – an identifying mark, symbol, word(s) or combination thereof that identifies one owner's products or services as distinct from another. ■ *Marketing* – a personality or image of a product or organisation in the minds of customers based on tangible and intangible attributes derived from promotion or usage. ■ *Accounting* – brands are part of the intangible assets and goodwill that can arise from an acquisition, and can be amortised over their useful economic lives (in the UK).

Challenger brand	A position taken by a brand and its owner as aiming to offer better value than the established leader in a given market space. This may manifest itself either as a serious contender for the top spot or by opportunistic jibes at the slower reaction times of the larger, more cumbersome leader.
Corporate identity	The sum of all the multimedia representations of a corporation, in both the physical and virtual worlds, that allows it to be clearly identified by its customers, business partners and employees. Visual components include colours, design, typeface, logo size and shape, etc.
Differentiators	Those facets of a brand that make it distinctive and facilitate choice between it and its competitors. Differentiators are normally articulated in marketing communications.
Endorsed brand	An endorsed brand usually takes the form of '(product name) by (personality)', where the personality is either a well-known individual or corporation. The endorsement by an individual plays on consumers' desires to emulate that person, while corporate endorsements are undertaken either to lend credibility or tie the individual product closer to its corporate owner.
Equity	Again, definitions vary. It can be expressed as an intangible – the strength of brand imagery in a person's mind. Alternatively, it is part of the goodwill of a corporation, in excess of its physical net assets, that contributes to the overall market value.
Essence/values	The core and soul of a brand, representing its single most valuable proposition in the minds – and hearts – of its users. Brand values are often expressed in a handful of key emotion-laden terms that support the brand essence.
Event brand	Functions or gatherings, usually within the worlds of entertainment or sport, that attract attention because of the participants or the audience or both. Often, the brand name of the event invokes images of the upper limits of human performance and creates anticipation for the next occurrence of the event.
Extension/leverage/ stretch	Moving the brand into new territory – product, service, geography, industry, etc. – to take advantage of the existing equity. If executed poorly, has the potential to inflict lasting brand damage.
Family of brands	The sum total of the master brand, sub-brands and related brands representing all products, services or delivery channels, often owned by the same parent. The master brand in this case is sometimes referred to as the umbrella brand and all the other brands as being part of the brand umbrella.
Geographic brand	The imagery associated with a particular location – ranging in size from a specific area through to an entire country. Normally, the smaller the area, the stronger the geographic brand.
Image/identity	The perception of the brand, in the minds of users, created through a combination of marketing communications issued by

the brand owner, coupled with the results of users' own interactions with the brand.

Lifestyle brand
Usually represents an aspiration of a style of living rather than a specific product or service.

Logo/logotype
A logo is a visual representation of a brand name while a logotype is the unique usage and grouping of letters that constitute the brand name.

Mapping
The process of analysing a brand to determine its positioning and ranking alongside other related brands, across a variety of criteria. Data to be used for the mapping process should include both factual and perceptual components.

Master brand
The principal, often original, and dominant brand possessed by an owner. The master brand may not be the largest direct contributor to an organisation's revenue or profits, but its indirect contribution, in the form of lending credibility to newer or sub-brands, is considerable.

Message
The key facets of a brand – real-world benefits, perceived values, future growth, etc. – that need to be communicated to relevant target audiences, including decision influencers such as the media.

Name creation
The process involving the identification, validation, visualisation and subsequent legal protection of a brand name, prior to its public release and usage.

Organisation brand
Usually the name of the organisation – or its public nickname – the organisation brand is used principally for corporate identification. If used for marketing communications, it is often presented as a master brand in its own right, bringing with it the might of the corporation it represents.

Orphan brand
An orphan brand is one that has fallen from greatness due to lack of investment, changing customer preferences or technological obsolescence.

Person brand
An individual who has achieved fame (or notoriety) – whether in the arena of business, sport, entertainment or politics – is identifiable as a person brand.

Personality/character
A brand is often marketed with, or acquires, human characteristics that allow it to transcend its physical product or service features, and make it more appealing to users.

Positioning
A brand's positioning aims to demarcate its territory, show how it squares up to its competitors and spell out what it represents to its users.

Product brand
Brands were originally created to distinguish the products of one owner from those of another, and product brands continue to play this role even today. Unaided recall of brands by consumers will invariably include names of product brands, given their longevity. Some product brands have also lent their name to the function their product performs, e.g. Xerox for photocopying.

Promise	Implicit in every brand interaction is a promise of the benefits that will accrue to users – whether tangible or intangible. Also known as the value proposition. The repeated failure to satisfy this promise will erode brand equity.
Range brand	A range brand works across a range of products, benefiting from economies of scale, and attempts to find synergies that raise the collective value of the brands included in the range.
Repertoire	Consumers do not necessarily identify with a single product in each product category – they have some alternatives within the repertoire from which they can choose.
Service brand	Service brands are difficult to create – and promote – given the absence of any physical attributes. However, with product innovations being copied increasingly quickly by competitors, it is possible that future marketing wars will be fought using service, rather than product, brands.
Share of voice	A measure of how the combination of messages and promotional expenditure compares with others in the same market space. Can be measured in terms of advertising spend or press column inches, or through more qualitative criteria. Share of voice should translate into share of mind (customer's perception and attention), which in turn should result in an increased share of market (increased sales).
Sister brand	Brands at an equal level within a single category are often referred to as sister brands.
Strategy	The brand strategy includes the vision for the brand and plans for how that vision is to be achieved over the medium and long terms. Details of the audiences – internal and external, customers and non-customers – and their intended brand experience will also be addressed.
Sub-brand	A sub-brand is one that sits under the master brand, from which it derives some of its leverage. The sub-brand's role is to extend the equity of the master brand, by exploring new product or service lines or even new distribution channels.
Visual identity	All the visual elements of a brand – its logo, typeface, size, colour, symbolism and packaging – that allow instant identification and differentiation from competitors.